Key Account Rock Stars

Key Account Rock Stars

Raising Your Volume by Lowering Your Decibels

Marc Pettersson

First published in 2024 by
Business Expert Press, LLC
222 East 46th Street, New York, NY 10017
www.businessexpertpress.com

ISBN-13: 978-1-63742-587-9 (paperback)
ISBN-13: 978-1-63742-588-6 (e-book)

Business Expert Press Selling and Sales Force Management Collection

First edition: 2024

10 9 8 7 6 5 4 3 2 1

Description

***Key Account Rock Stars: Raising Your Volume by Lowering Your Decibels* brings fresh new thoughts to the topic of key account management.**

This book reveals the secrets of how to successfully engage with customers and how to become organizationally savvy, plus practical tools for succeeding on the job. It is written for the practitioner and takes the readers through the soft sides of the job, which is exactly what is needed to succeed and achieve career fulfillment.

Account managers must keep relationships fresh, with creative ways to add value to the customers, so customers remain genuinely satisfied with the relationship. Losing a customer will always be a burden on the individual key account manager, whatever the reason for the loss.

Readers will:

- Gain awareness of what a good customer relationship looks like
- Learn tools to solve issues and improve ways of working
- **Most importantly, learn how to succeed as a key account manager**

Remember, the importance of customer centricity is higher than ever. The decade-long transition of the economy away from production toward services and the need to differentiate from the competition will certainly continue. **Today, a company that fails to engage with the customers will not succeed; the era of making a good product and trusting it to sell itself is long gone.**

Keywords

key account management activities; key account management best practices; key account management for dummies; key account management negotiation skills; key account management B2B; career advice for key account managers; soft skills for key account managers; negotiation skills for key account managers; strategic account management; large customer sales; account-based marketing

Contents

Acknowledgments

A big thanks to BEP for their vision to publish this book and for faith in my abilities as an author. And to all those real rock stars who supported me on the way, making this book what it is—specifically, those who were willing to be interviewed and provided insight into their experiences and accumulated know-how:

Philippe Aba—Global Client Director, Celonis

Raphael Asseo—Partner, Page Executive

Ohad Goldberg—Company President, AstraZeneca Israel

Csaba Holop—Global Business Director, Celanese

Martin Kruczinna—Chief Executive Officer, Pearl Group

Hanjun Kwon—Senior Director, Global Key Account Management, Entegris

Walid Masrouha—Business Applications Specialist, Microsoft

Colleen Nichol—Senior Partner Account Manager, Salesforce

Thierry Prédhom—Solution Sales Manager and Event Manager, Camptocamp

Vanessa Smets—Key Account Management Strategist and Business Storyteller, Skyguide

Marije van Weelden—Coach and Managing Director, Apotheek Ermel

Ronald Wintzéus—Principal and Managing Director, Pullman Group and Eames Wyatt

Loreta Berhami—Publishing Director for Botime Pegi and General Manager for ESDP, who mentored me through writing and publishing. She gave me courage to pursue writing when I thought of quitting.

Maggie Lyons—Editor, freelance, for structuring my thoughts, challenging the unclear parts of the book, and, overall, improving the work tremendously.

Introduction

This book is a practical guide for practitioners, written by a practitioner. I worked as a key account (KA) manager for several years and loved the job for its variety, business challenges, and opportunities to learn something new every day.

What surprised me was the lack of information that would help me do the job, the small but important nuggets that make a huge difference between being a bland employee and a rock star. I felt that having to make every mistake by myself was a missed opportunity, knowing that others before me must have gone through a similar experience of trial and error.

Much good material is available on the topic of key account management (KAM), but it is mostly targeted at corporate leaders in its focus on the mechanics of creating a KAM department. This kind of literature is mostly about how to measure success, useful tools and templates, structuring the department, selecting key accounts, and how to make the corporation efficient in this field. What I was looking for was something more personalized, more about using technical and, particularly, *soft skills* that would help me to successfully negotiate the everyday technical and, especially, human challenges of the job, which, in turn, would help promoting my career.

Learning on the job is expensive. Asking stupid questions and making mistakes are welcomed in the beginning but, as time goes on, less acceptable. So when I changed career paths, I decided to make a note of some of the insights I wish I'd had to begin with, intangible parts of the job that are critical to KAM success.

What is KAM? Several good definitions exist, and I have selected three that give a rounded view. The widely used definition is by Malcolm McDonald and Beth Rogers, scholars in the field of KAM and sales:

> *An approach to strategic customers (whose needs you need to understand in depth), which offers them value that distinguishes you from your competitors.*[1]

---

[1] M. McDonald and B. Rogers. 2017. *On Key Account Management* (London: Kogan Page), p. 2.

Their definition has the clear focus on understanding the customer with the scope of gaining competitive advantage. They continue further by stating that the essence is how to devote the scarce business resources effectively.

However, there are also alternative views. Tim Hughes and Matt Reynolds, who are thought leaders in the field of sales, define KAM as:

> *A strategic approach to business marketing in which an organization considers and communicates with individual prospects or customer accounts as markets of one.*[2]

I like it because Hughes and Reynolds are marketing focused and, from their perspective, the term *account-based marketing* (ABM) is a synonym for KAM. In general, this is not the case, and ABM differs from KAM. It is a marketing approach where marketing activities are tailored to specific customers. This is as opposed to traditional marketing where a broader range of prospective customers are being targeted with the same activities.

The successful application of ABM is complementing KAM and is suitable for companies that have a certain maturity in marketing, innovation, and business intelligence. It can be seen as a layer on top of a functioning KAM structure. For me, this definition emphasizes the need to think beyond sales.

My preferred definition would be the one of Gartner:

> *Key account management (KAM) is the process of planning and managing a mutually beneficial partnership between an organization and its most important customers.*[3]

It is important to keep in mind that the motive for a company to create a KAM function is because they believe there will be a positive payback. The company will invest in the relationship by prioritizing these specific customers above others. They don't do it out of altruism; there has to be a positive outcome for it to make business sense. Hence, not all

---

[2] T. Hughes and M. Reynolds. 2016. *Social Selling* (London: Kogan Page), p. 53.
[3] Gartner. 2022. "Key Account Management," *Sales Glossary.*

companies see the need for a KAM function. And indeed, many companies do not need a KAM program at all. It carries costs to have one, and more importantly, it adds complexity to managing a company. It is more voices to an already crowded table of decision makers. And more points for tension inside the organization if not orchestrated very skillfully.

This question is asked regularly by leadership teams. According to a Gartner study, almost 70 percent of organizations surveyed had rebuilt

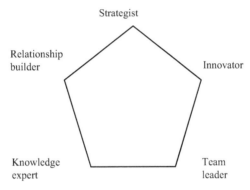

Figure A.1 The dimensions of the key account management function. A full toolbox of skills is needed to master the job

their KAM programs in the past seven years due to underperformance. Almost half of the companies had rebuilt twice or more. Additionally, the same study showed that three-quarters of KA managers thought their organizational practices were inefficient at growing the partnerships.[4] This means that establishing a KAM program is far from easy, and there is no right way to do it. And it also means that the individual KA manager will go through a reorganization every few years.

In the following table are some of the activities that a typical KA manager will perform. They are divided into processes and ad hoc activities. Processes are activities that recur and can be, to some extent, standardized, documented, and usually planned. The ad hoc activities are unplanned and are so new in content that experiences from past activities are not fully transferable. It is worth noting, projects can be managed

---

[4] Gartner. October 21, 2021. *(Rebuilding) Key Account Programs for Growth*, p. 5.

Processes That Involve the KA Manager	Ad Hoc Activities
Negotiations	Special projects
New business development	Nonstandard production constraints, resource requests, or senior management involvement
Innovation events	Customer information requests
Payment or credit issues	Request from customers for collaboration on strategic activities, specific networking events, trade fairs, and marketing
Quality issues	Strategic events in the industry; mergers, reorganizations, bankruptcies
Supplier performance management processes	
Managing contract disputes	
Demand–supply issues	

using standardized project management tools, despite the different content, teams, and scope.

A successful KA manager will interact with a range of people in the customer organization. There is usually a main counterpart that works for the part of the organization that is responsible for strategic supply, whatever that will be called—procurement, sourcing, or something else, as the name might be used differently. It can also be interacting directly with a business function. Either way, you hope to be part of the group of selected few suppliers who are, formally or informally, considered strategic and important for the customer. In cases where the interaction is with persons responsible only for the operative part of purchasing goods, then, clearly, you are not as key to them as they are to you. And your life will be harder.

In many cases, there is considerable interaction with other teams, specifically the technology departments for software suppliers, operations for industrial suppliers, Human Resources for recruiters, and so on—and then a myriad of other contacts on a more or less regular basis.

For this book, I will not put too much emphasis on who exactly is the main contact; it is not that important. The term procurement will be used from here on for the function that strategically manages important suppliers, contracts, businesses, major quality issues, and important activities outside the day-to-day activities. The day-to-day work is usually done directly by the local teams of the two companies.

The commercial field has many roles to offer, of which KA manager is one. For anyone new to the field interested in starting a career, it is fundamental to understand the differences between the different roles. Each has very different characteristics and requires different skills to succeed.

- *Sales*: Hands-on work, competitive as success is measured based on immediate and tangible results. It is often tactical in nature as predominately the leads are selected by someone else and the products and services offered clearly defined before engaging with customers, A hunter mentality is required and the roles are often associated with extrovert personalities, A desire for winning will make the job more motivating.
- *Business development*: More intellectual in nature, suitable for someone who likes exploring unknown areas. A focus on partnering rather than transactions and the scope is rather strategic. Creativity is required to find ways of entering new markets, defining what to offer the customers, and identifying new customer journeys. Includes plenty of research.
- *Account management*: Relationship focused, with a long-term time horizon. Win–win mentality is fundamental, as the customers need to be retained. A farmer mindset, nurturing the accounts to ensure that the relationship flourish over a long period of time. Strategic in nature, with a larger part of the time spent negotiating, collaborating, and solving problems for the customers.

In reality, the boundaries between roles are fluid and each industry and company will apply the role terminology differently. Still for a genuine KA manager role, the main part of the job should be farming current customers, with a minor hunter component for gaining new business with existing customers, regaining lost customers, or hunting for new customers. The ratio depends on the job, which will dictate what kind of candidate is suitable. Someone with a strong hunter instinct will need a role where the new customer component is large, while a farmer will be very suitable for a role taking care of the top customers of a company with multiyear contracts and little room to expand.

Fundamentally, the scope of the key account function is to create stronger relations with existing customers. Each key customer has a designated KA manager responsible for this partnership. Channeling the interactions and managing the touchpoints between the customer and supplier aim at creating a smoother and higher-quality engagement for both partners. The challenges and demands of the job are broad, and the KA manager's skill set for this task needs to be up to the task. More about this in the last chapter.

This book offers you my insights and experience, plus valuable advice from a variety of sources, with the scope of developing tools needed for success in the role. The book will be quite North-America and Europe-centric, as my experience is mostly in these areas. This is not to diminish the existence of all the regions not covered, just that as the book is based on my insights, it would not be right to claim expertise in these geographies. What is written might apply to other countries or not.

The following are a few books that present a different view and that I have found useful. See the bibliography for full publication details.

- Woodburn, Diana and McDonald, Malcolm, *Key Account Management: The Definitive Guide.* The comprehensive guide to creating and developing a KAM structure. Textbook for academia, consulting, and senior management.
- Cheverton, Peter, *Key Account Management: Tools and Techniques for Achieving Profitable Key Supplier Status.* "A complete action kit of tools and techniques for achieving profitable key supplier status" says it all. This is as much of a reference work as the previous one—especially good for anyone new to the topic; these are the two books to start with.
- Hennessey, H. David and Jeannet, Jean-Pierre, *Global Account Management: Creating Value.* A very solid and comprehensive guide to the strategic side of global account management.
- Shankar, Bala, *Nuanced Account Management: Driving Excellence in B2B Sales.* Information-packed book with genuine insights and a clear view of the challenges of the job. One of

my favorites, as Shankar shows that he knows what the job is really about and has the capacity to capture the essence of it.

- Stewart, Grant, *Successful Key Account Management in a Week: Teach Yourself*. Nice summary of the main KAM tools.

More books are listed in the bibliography, each with a different viewpoint to help build a balanced and powerful insight into KAM.

CHAPTER 1

Know Them as You Know Yourself

Overview

- Understand what it means to own the customer relationship and to be a thought leader within your organization.
- Get close to your main counterpart, the buyer, who represents the customer's procurement team. This person will likely be the main contact in the customer organization, so the relationship needs to be strong.
- Network your way to success. Learn from Keith Ferrazzi on how to farm the field so that your network is healthy when you need it.
- Learn the secrets of business intelligence and how to use Michael Porter's five forces approach. A strategic mindset enables a KA manager to understand the landscape in which they operate.
- Digital tools for customer engagement play a strong role in KAM and they blend together with traditional in-person interaction.

A Great Customer Relationship

Owning a customer relationship—being insightful about the customer's business; having a broad, industry-relevant network; and having an overall understanding of what makes the customer tick.

It is more than capabilities. It is capabilities and attitude that will boost your value with your customers and the company you work for and increase your personal status as a rock star KA manager. A thought leader and customer advocate is genuinely passionate about the customer. Knowing the customer's history helps, as will an excellent network for gaining industry insight, and a few other tools that will help gain the status as a sought-after customer expert.

But, first, a few words about your counterpart, the buyer, who works for procurement. The role of the buyer is, to some extent, a mirror of the KA manager. Procurement sees the world through the lens of product categories. It evaluates how critical a certain category is for its business. If the category is business critical, there are only one or a few suppliers, and there are risks involved, then it would be good to find a strategic partner who will prioritize the relationship and ensure supply. In a situation like this, procurement would be very happy to gain key account status from the supplier. This is a good match for both the supplier and the customer. However, if procurement considers the category a commodity with little supply risks, then it will try to put as little effort as possible into it and classify this category as a "nuisance."[1] Try to be a KA manager to a customer who considers you a nuisance; that is not an easy life.

As the KA manager, the buyer has a big internal team of stakeholders to orchestrate. While the KA manager wants to expand the connection to have multiple touchpoints and a strong network within the customer's organization, the buyers usually prefer to keep the interactions controlled through them. So rule number one is not to try to step on the buyer's toes and bypass them. You need to stay on good terms, or the doors will start to close for you in the customer's organization.

The decision-making process of changing suppliers or allocating more business, especially in strategic categories, will be complex and depend as much on their risk management as your sales pitch.

This is important to keep in mind when networking and pitching business to a customer.

The Go-To Person

The thought leader is a go-to person: someone the company looks to when difficult tasks need to be undertaken. This person is a collaborator who is appreciated for sharing generously, which brings value to the company's network. This does not mean being indispensable. People who

---

[1] P. Kraljic. September 1983. "Purchasing Must Become Supply Management," Harvard Business Review.

set out to be indispensable build fortresses in a futile attempt to make the company operate around them. This won't happen. Well-operated companies are built on a stronger and more durable material than a single person. By organizational design, there should be no irreplaceable persons in a public company. Important and difficult to replace people, yes for sure but beyond that will cripple any organization.

The stunned look of people who have been terminated shows that they thought the company would never let them go as they had made their positions as irreplaceable as they could. But organizations don't grind to a halt due to one person, not even when teams depart. A KA manager that rises above the company will be a risk. In specific industries where the dealmaking is based on complex personal relations and connections, there are individuals who have disproportional influence on the customer; in certain sectors and geographies, this is very common. It makes business sense to pay millions to someone who has access to doors otherwise closed.

If you don't carry an address book with the names of presidents, celebrities, and CEOs, or have a royal title, then strive toward becoming a go-to person instead.

You want to be more than merely the one who knows the most about the customer; you should also possess insight into a larger space. This could be the larger customer segment, industry, procurement model, products, or geography, for example. And you should do this without losing your focus on the core competence: the customer.

Your knowledge is an important resource. Share your technical expertise, industry vertical insight, or whatever is interesting to you and valuable to a broader community. Your unique personal brand is not only relevant internally within your company but, as it is highly transferable, will also serve you well beyond your current KA manager position. Insights and opinions are not reserved for the top management and, when you actively share this knowledge with external partners, it will enforce your employer's brand too. Communicate your knowledge and insights beyond the company and customer space for the good of the industry. This practice is perfected by entrepreneurs, so learn from these gurus. Experts on LinkedIn, Instagram, and so on have tools and tricks you can learn from. However, it is not about shouting out your insights but about building credibility. It is about subtly conveying your capabilities to those who are interested. Keeping your decibels down will make a stronger impact in the long run.

To achieve this, you will require insight, a capability for analytics and synthesis, and crisp communication skills, a topic I explore further in Chapter 8, "Keep It Simple."

Because digital marketing is a major tool for scaling your voice and forming connections, it is worth having a look at *Social Selling* by Tim Hughes and Matt Reynolds. Choosing the right tools depends on your industry and where your customers are. LinkedIn and X (Twitter) are the tools of choice for Tim and Matt and are, at this moment of writing, the most used tools globally. Sharing your valuable insights and those of others by writing, analyzing, and summarizing—especially summarizing information into a more digestible, visual form—are great ways to add value to your network.

Take extra care to be efficient with this type of sharing. Letting it dominate your work as a KA manager will alienate your current customers and distract you from dealing with the everyday challenges of your work.

Learn from the best:

1. *Simon Sinek* created his own movement for inspiration and optimism and is a great example of how to become a thought leader without a traditional path in the specific field and with no academic background. Writing books helps but is not required. Good material and a clear area of expertise are what counts.[2]
2. *Tim Ferris* is full of energy and curiosity. Take a look at how he writes. It is very distinctive.[3]
3. *Nancy Nardin* focuses on tools to improve sales, combining sales and technology, and offering engaging material for a KA manager.[4]

---

[2] The Optimism Company from Simon Sinek. https://simonsinek.com (accessed March 2, 2024).

[3] T. Ferriss. 2022. *The Tim Ferriss Show.* https://tim.blog/ (accessed March 2, 2024).

[4] N. Nardin. 2022. *"SalesTech Landscape" (graphic) and Complete Guide to SalesTech.* https://www.youtube.com/c/NancyNardin (accessed March 2, 2024).

4. *Trish Bertuzzi* is the go-to author on business-to-business tools, focusing on inside sales. She gives great advice and combines a direct sales approach with empathy and situational awareness.[5]

5. *Brian Burns* is a business-to-business sales expert, with the right lingo for his target group of sales professionals. With sharp and accurate comments, he has created a clear space for his expertise. He is especially creative in his informative short videos, featuring himself on the phone with fictional counterparts.[6]

If you decide to start to make a name for yourself online, avoid at all costs lamely reposting your company's official posts, peppered with your own comments that shout fake excitement. That is a turnoff. So, be genuine and post topics that interest you and at least some other people. You don't have to generate a massive audience. In this field, it is more important to attract a narrower but deeper group of followers.

Make Your Contact Your Spokesperson

One crucial role of the procurement team is to sell its decisions within its own company. It evaluates new options, changes suppliers, and tenders new opportunities on a regular basis, all of which have, in addition to strategic impact, a major operational impact on its business. Examples of operational impact are numerous: (1) The people involved in day-to-day operations will have to make changes if a new supplier is introduced. (2) The product development team will have additional constraints on its choices if the procurement team limits the choice of suppliers. (3) The supply chain management must rewire its network, and the back office teams need to set up new accounts. As with any change, there will be resistance, and some people will be more satisfied than others with the new solution.

When resistance happens, the procurement team faces the task of explaining and convincing its stakeholders of the choices it has made. The

---

[5] T. Bertuzzi. 2022. *The Bridge Group*. www.bridgegroupinc.com/trish-bertuzzi (accessed February 28, 2024).

[6] B.G. Burns. 2022. *B2B Revenue Leadership*. www.b2brevenue.com (accessed March 16, 2024).

secret here is that, even if your company is the winner of a deal, your procurement counterpart at the customer company is unlikely to share these challenges with you. Sharing too openly will show their vulnerability and reveal the fact that they will act as a spokesperson for your company as soon as the deal they made is signed.

To manage this double role, your counterpart will need to switch roles, from that of a tough buyer to that of a passionate cheerleader for your company and the deal they signed with you. You and your sales team will not be aware of this double role and will rarely face it directly. To get at least a glimpse of it, try to get into meetings and discussions where your procurement contacts and their co-workers are present to see how their relationship works. This will show the discussions behind the curtains and the challenges the procurement team faces. For example, someone on their team has strong objections on a technical point that you might be able to resolve. Or they had a strong collaboration for years with another supplier, so you will need to win them over.

Regardless of whether you are being made aware of such challenges or not, it is in your best interest to help your counterpart with this task. Sabotaging them in their internal pitching will make them an enemy for life.

There are many ways of supporting them:

- *Communicate clearly*: Prepare communications (e-mail, presentations, and offers) that can be shared easily by your counterpart with their own stakeholders. A clear graph will be easy for them to copy and share, rather than something full of jargon or lacking the full story.
- *Notice resistance*: Become aware of the resistance they are facing from other departments, so look carefully for signs of this. For example, you observe an awkward conversation between the product development lead and procurement about a feature. You sense that there are topics that have not been overtly shared and that, below the surface, you face resistance from the product development lead. Possibly they have needs that your company can't fully address,

resulting in frustration. With large accounts, this will often occur.

- *Be businesslike*: Keep your communication at a professional level. Don't become too intimate with the procurement team, which might raise suspicion that procurement is not acting independently. However close your actual relationship is, it is better to have it look professional and not too cozy.
- *Share insights*: Provide information on the product, production methods, and industry, so procurement can shine when sharing this with its own company.

Some salespeople have the tendency to vent their frustration after facing challenges with a customer. This is understandable as they likely took a beating and couldn't push back. They share their pent-up frustration vocally with their co-workers. This may help them feel better, and then, they forget about it. However, the audience within their company will likely remember what they said and form their perception of the customer accordingly. The one-sided narrative about the customer, told in a moment of frustration, lingers on and affects the sales team's motivation to support this customer.

It's better to keep these recounts within a close, trusted, team. For the rest of the company, promote a storyline that reflects how the customer is 99 percent of the time.

Network as a Movie Star

There are no shortcuts to gaining earth-shattering networking results, and your own personality is the starting point. Some people are natural at achieving results quickly and efficiently. For the rest, it's about working hard and systematically to get the desired results.

Forming new relationships and managing current ones are musts for anyone in sales. For a KA manager in particular, the focus is on nurturing existing relationships, as opposed to acquiring new ones. Forming new relationships within the existing customer's company is much easier than acquiring new customers.

The basics of networking with new people can be summarized in about four rules:

1. *Offer support*: Networking is more like farming or gardening than hunting.[7] Likely, it will take patience to plant the seeds for potential future benefits. And networking should be seen as a way to support a community, not as working a transactional marketplace. Your best approach is to have something you can share with others. For example, the thought-leadership status you have created is a natural way of creating value for others.

2. *Focus on listening*: Listen with genuine interest, as opposed to pitching the sale. Nobody wants to hear a generic sales pitch or a monolog for long. Keep in mind that value has to be created for more people than yourself. If you take a one-sided approach to networking, it clearly will not be sustainable.

3. *Exit gracefully*: There's no need to worry. You will not find compatibility with everybody. Move on politely when the conversation is stuck or you feel excluded from the conversation or the topic does not interest you.

4. *Study the best*: Practice makes perfect. Learn how to network from the best. There are many small tricks to learn, including the art of people-reading, and they all require practice. Also, fear of speaking with strangers, fear of rejection, and the pressure of making conversations will make networking challenging.

The approach you take will depend on what you wish to gain: short-term contacts or a deeper connection with some specific person.

Just as negotiations, sales, or any other human engagements are, networking is based on subtleties in the way we interact, and the more we are exposed to it, the easier it will get.

Keith Ferrazzi, author of the bestseller *Never Eat Alone*, takes that approach and does so on steroids. He is a master networker who attributes

---

[7] The Art of Charm (professional and personal coaching service). n.d. "The Art of Networking for Introverts," Interview with Karen Wickre, *YouTube Video Series, Episode 784*. www.youtube.com/watch?v=V6SjIkUxpO4.

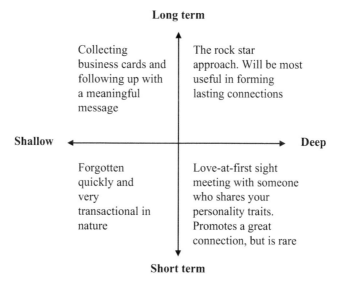

Figure 1.1 Choose the way to network based on your needs. Every event can have different needs

a lot of his success to the work he has put into networking. Keith emphasizes having the mindset of helping others without a specific need in mind. "Business cycles ebb and flow; your friends and trusted associates remain." So, for networking,

- *Bring something to the party:* It could be energy, discussions, or insight.
- *Don't gossip*: It's better to have information of value or valuable opinions. Gossipers seldom gain the respect of others.
- *Volunteer*: Take part in building your community as a way to superconnect and gain access to many participants.
- *Create your personal brand*: This means sharing your expertise generously and having the courage to stand out.
- *Tailor your approach*: Familiarize yourself with the attendees so you can prepare for conversations with people you are specifically interested in connecting with.
- *Prepare well*: The word *work* in *networking* is there for a reason. The more you are prepared, the better the results. Preparing can be scrolling the attendee list, finding interesting people and companies, and contacting the organizers in

advance. The organizers are putting in the hard work to make the event happen. Be grateful and support them in making the event highly successful.

- *Exit options*: Have clear exit options for leaving discussions that are not working. Going for a drink is a worn excuse, as is the bathroom card, so use them sparingly. It's better to be frank: "I'm looking for someone I wanted to meet, and I think they are here now. But let's continue this discussion later." If you find yourself in a position where you are excluded from the conversation, smooth backstepping and exiting with a nod and smile works perfectly.

- *Manage your discomfort*: I get restless at events. Remembering names is a challenge and too many signals make my brain so hyperactive that it's impossible to focus. I struggle to follow a conversation. On several occasions, I have asked the same questions repeatedly. It can happen to anyone. Just accept that you will have to manage the situation, especially if you are introverted and not comfortable with meeting people you don't know well or don't know at all.

- *Follow up*: The small effort of following up has a major impact. Try to think of ways to be creative in the follow-up message.

Mapping the Landscape

It is important to know the industry of both your company and your customer. They are not the same. Avoid the trap of thinking that because you know your business, you will also know theirs. Learning about both requires having a helicopter view to see the big picture without distractions.

Having an understanding of both industries brings major advantages. As most people don't have in-depth knowledge of more than their own industry, your insights into both your customer's business and your own company's business will help you stand out. It's the language of true leaders. Here's an example:

The CEO and cofounder of a construction supplies company was extremely passionate about his company and industry. To be up-to-date with the competition, he collected competitors' annual reports that were available in print. He laid them out on a separate table in his office and encouraged anyone entering his office to browse through them and offer any insights they might have after reading them. He saw these annual reports as a secret source, meant for others but available to him, to enrich his industry knowledge.

A good tool to start with is Porter's five forces analysis. This is one of the very few tools in the book, despite my claim in the introduction that this book would not be about tools and templates. The reason for choosing this is the value to the KA manager. Despite it losing popularity lately, probably because it fits badly with the flow of a PowerPoint presentation, the value of seeing the business through this lens makes the KA manager more attuned to how the company leadership thinks. The tool is a strategy framework developed by professor Michael Porter in 1979. It has a few disadvantages worth pointing out: (1) It does not reflect the technology changes since 1979 and (2) it does not cover the topic of regulation very well. But it is universal and broad enough to use for the purpose here: to understand the competitive environment.[8]

- *New entrants*: If a market is attractive, new companies will
  continue to enter it, offering the same products or something
  better. New entrants are often hungrier and more agile. A
  new entrant can upset the balance and force changes on
  stable industries where competing companies are few and
  have established technology. A new entrant may capture
  a regulatory agency and externally impose changes on
  the industry. If the industry is heavily influenced by this

[8] M. Porter. April 1979. "How Competitive Forces Shape Strategy," Harvard Business Review.

regulatory capture, it's better to focus on the regulations specifically.

- *The strength of the suppliers*: The suppliers, in this case you and your competitors, can have significant power. Intel is the best example of a component manufacturer that managed to gain significant market power and even develop a brand among the end users. When companies in commoditized businesses command a strong technical position (e.g., know-how or patents), the suppliers might be forced to compete on price alone without the benefit of other resources. You ought to be very aware of how easy it would be for the customer to replace your product with a substitute.

- *Your customers' edge*: How much say do your customers have with their respective customers? Brand value, technical position, and where they distribute their goods determine how easy it would be for their customers to replace their products with substitutes. Customer losses can also be due to a product that is good to have rather than essential. Crocs, for example, held a strong position vis-à-vis their competitors, with no direct threat of substitute products, but the company's growth stopped when customers lost interest in the product. In addition, events that change the balance, such as acquisitions and new technology, can explain why a company is not making money or desperately seeking new innovations or tough on suppliers.

- *Substitutions*: A leather supplier will compete not only with other makers of leather but also with synthetic materials, which makes the competitive space much more complex. The risk is that someone revolutionizes the whole business and makes current players irrelevant or small changes in behavior change the demand for a product or service. The substitute can be as simple as going to the movie theater instead of a restaurant, but if enough people do it, it will influence the business. For example, in the United Kingdom, a long

cultural tradition of going for a few after-work drinks to
the local pub has been declining lately. Between 2000 and
2020, close to a quarter of all pubs closed. Several factors
contributed to the decline; most of them were because
the customers substituted the pub with something else,
channeling their time and money to other businesses. Many
cut back on their consumption of alcohol by pursuing
healthier activities such as going to the gym instead of going
to the pub for a pint.[9] Another common type of substitution
is new technology that disrupts the industry. For many
industries, the risk of losing customers from revolutionary
new technology makes this disruptor very powerful.

- *Rivalry*: Rivalry refers to how the customer company is
  positioned among its own competitors. You, as a supplier,
  have an excellent insight if your company is supplying several
  of the key players in the specific industry. This is often the
  case, especially if your products or services competitive and
  you have a large market share. W.L. Gore & Associates
  probably have some of the best insights into the premium
  segment outdoors clothing market as they are the producer of
  Gore-Tex fabric. They see how each clothing brand performs
  and how they operate as businesses. This insight is very hard
  to replicate for an outsider. And likely, you won't have all the
  insight, but your colleagues likely will. Understanding who
  is successful and who is struggling is a good starting point.
  Cultural differences in their operations and comparisons of
  their various metrics will show that they all have different
  ways of working. If they are business-to-consumer companies,
  you might experience their offering directly or someone close
  to you does.

---

[9] N. Foley. July 2, 2019. "Last Orders? The Decline of Pubs Around the UK,"
House of Commons Library.

What is happening in the industry will start to make sense when you have this kind of insight. There are many other ways to view the market. None of them depend on the tools you use but, rather, on your curiosity to see beyond the obvious. You have to be a spy and an investigative journalist, and enough information is available in the public space that you should not be tempted to break the law or flout ethical principles. For example, if a customer shares confidential information with you, or you have confidential information about your company that is not public, then you should keep such matters strictly to yourself. The rules should be clear. Many resources are available to guide you on legal and ethical issues and, in doing so, gain the respect of the business community. If in doubt, speak to your company lawyer.[10]

Within these limits, everything is possible. Your insightful conversations with senior managers and other industry thought leaders will become much more rewarding. You don't need to be a management consultant to see trends or risks. What you need is a bit of original insight, something customers can't see from their perspective. Sharing it with them gives them something of value.

How do you know if you are a thought leader? It is not the number of LinkedIn followers or the number of conferences you participate in. It is the simple fact that you get invited by the customer—invited to innovation events, to opening of factories, to meet people in their organization, and to share your opinion. You will feel that they value and trust you. And you will see that you spend more and more time with them on increasingly critical issues, helping their business.

Your feedback counts, and the effort you have put in to build a trusting relationship, honesty, integrity and insight will start to show. And you will start to get more and more relevant and honest feedback, which is fuel for improvements. Suppliers in relationships lacking trust are cut off from the thoughts and opinions of the customer. Why would they share information about their business to a supplier with whom they have a distant relationship.

---

[10] SCIP (Strategic and Competitive Intelligence Professionals) offers a business code of ethics at www.scip.org/page/Ethical-Intelligence.

Picture this: A young-looking female key account manager in the payment industry faced the challenge of convincing middle-aged, male chief financial officers of large retail chains that she knew her stuff. With the power of business intelligence and storytelling, she came to the meeting.

Before stepping into those high-stakes meetings, she went above and beyond the average research, delving into the financial and economic circumstances of each of the chains of the group and understanding their pain points, challenges, and opportunities. Armed with this knowledge, she transformed from just another salesperson to a strategic partner who truly understood their business.

And she didn't stop there; when she walked with these CFOs to the meeting room, she steered clear of idle small talk about the weather. Instead, she asked a few pointed questions about their business. This wasn't just a ploy; it was a genuine effort to establish a solid baseline and show them that she was invested in their success. Needless to say, she earned their respect.

When you have developed a good insight into the customer space, your focus should turn to how well you manage to connect and drive the relationship forward without falling into the traps that commonly plague a close supplier–customer relationship.

The Pandemic Path to Digital Transformation

When the COVID-19 pandemic hit the world in 2020 and many countries limited mobility, companies had to adapt quickly. Business moved online overnight, with commercial work changing drastically. Business could continue, helped by communication tools that had been profiteering for over a decade before the outbreak. Videoconferencing soon became the surrogate for any meeting. Despite well-working technology and Internet connections, the experience was not even remotely as good as face-to-face meetings, as many KA managers already knew.

The shift online downshifted formality in business; working from an improvised home workstation meant that children, pets, partners, and all other external actors became part of the meetings. Dress codes were relaxed. Something that could have been seen as unprofessional before the epidemic now received compassion; everybody was in the same situation. So, in many industries, customer meetings took a more casual tone. And without a polished professional appearance, the human behind the role appeared, making small talk more tangible. Talking about one's family during a coffee break is different from seeing the family on the screen, in their home.

At the same time, a generational shift is slowly taking place, with younger professionals who are much more comfortable with digital channels. Gartner reports that already up to 80 percent of B2B decision makers prefer remote human interaction or digital self-service. Though we are speaking of sales, not KAM, the interaction between KA managers and buyers before the pandemic was likely of those proportions already, with in-person interaction counting for less than 20 percent of total engagement. However, quantity is not quality. Any KA manager knows that an excellent meeting will be groundbreaking and worth the time.

The videoconferencing tools that boomed during the restrictions proved sticky, and they took a generational step forward in terms of quality and functionality, improving the user experience. And they became permanently ingrained into the work routines, remained after the restrictions were lifted, became a stronger part of work routines, and reduced the number of meetings. The time saved from reducing business travel made many companies decide to drastically reduce in-person customer meetings. The loss of quality was compensated by much more efficient use of time. In some industries, for example, software and international business, where workers were spread over different global locations, the step to becoming almost exclusively digital was small.

In addition to web conferencing, all the other digital tools supporting commercial activities took a step forward. Data became more dynamic and the tools refined. Data dominate modern society, even in KAM, which is a bastion of personal relationships. Gartner expects a big shift in the coming years that will transition the sales universe from experience- and intuition-based to data-driven selling. Realistic demos, better webpages, webinars, and self-service interfaces have become standard. The self-service aspect proved to be a winning concept as this gives the buyer more control of their schedule and attention.[11] Information is best transferred like this, avoiding friction and delays. Most companies are experts in tracking and storing data, while making it digestible and available at the right moment is still challenging. That is where the value of a great KA manager comes in. People strongly prefer relationships with people; people love people, not computers.[12]

Face-to-face meetings usually contain slack, unscheduled time when the participants can chat or discuss other business. This valuable interaction is removed as videoconferences allow for much more structured time. The schedule is controlled and it is very difficult to get a natural conversation going. Less spontaneous calls happened, and activities got scheduled as people took comfort in the feeling of control. Sitting at home, able to pin every activity into the calendar in 45-minute slots proved to be like cocaine for the human brain. The classical call of just ringing the customer decreased and mutated into a prearranged video call.

There is an indication that some of the interaction with customers has moved to trade fairs and conferences, with companies seeing it as a way to make travel more efficient; it is possible to combine many visits over a few days. This sense of efficiency fitted well with the realization of how much waste there was in business travel.

Summary

A great KA manager is insightful about the customer's business, has a strong and extensive network within the industry, and understands the customer. These capabilities are very valuable to the company. This manager is then a go-to person who is sought out for expertise in their specific niche.

A thought leader and customer advocate is genuinely passionate about their customers. They know the customer's history, possess excellent

---

[11] Gartner. 2020. *The Future of Sales, Transformational Strategies for B2B Sales Organizations*, pp. 2–8.

[12] S. Van Belleghem. 2015. *Digital Becomes Human* (Croydon: Kogan Page), pp. 92–97, 152.

networking skills, and actively help others. Managing the relationship with the customer's procurement counterpart, the buyer, is crucial and forms a base for all engagement and activity. It will be difficult to make any impact if this relationship is not working well.

Networking is a vital aspect of the KA manager's role, and it requires patience and skills to get results from it. Having clear expectations of what to get of it and focusing on listening while avoiding pitching the company or product are important. There are tools to make the most out of it, which helps to become a better networker.

The KA manager's role is strategic, and to succeed in the role, you need an understanding of the industry's competitive landscape of both the customer's and the KA manager's companies. Porter's five forces analysis can help to gain insights into the industry and identify potential risks and opportunities.

By combining insightful conversations with industry leaders, honest feedback, and continuous efforts to build trust, the KA manager can establish themselves as a trusted strategic partner to the customer. Such a relationship fosters collaboration, growth, and mutual success.

CHAPTER 2

The Relationship Trap

Overview

- Being close to the buyer is a must, but being too close leads to problems. The days of wine and dine are gone in most industries.
- Expanding your network and understanding the role of invisible stakeholders.
- Communicating with confidence, remaining honest, being present, and keeping a healthy distance from the issues take the KA manager a long way when it comes to engaging with the customer.

Customer Intimacy

The closeness of your relationship with the customer can cause a variety of pitfalls that can jeopardize the good work of building the relationship and complicate your job.

KA managers are here for the long run. Signing new contracts or seeing a streak of growing sales is rewarding, but the game plan is to keep the customer loyal and stable for years. Retaining a business-to-business customer requires a different approach from acquiring new customers or satisfying a business-to-consumer customer.

In addition to the supplier's provision of superior products and services, the way the KA manager manages the relationship will affect the outcome. The account manager can, for example, take a personal approach where the relationship is maintained through the use of wine and dine tactics, freebies, and personal favors. This approach is opaque, so there is the risk that someone else forms a better relationship with the customer and takes the business away. Going solo is not the way to go; even rock stars need a supporting band to shine.

A strategic approach will be a good complement and is the opposite of a personal approach; the KA manager works to improve the business and modus operandi, using analytics, systems, and processes to improve the customer experience.

Reliance on a single contact is expanded to more contact points between the customer and the supplier. As will be explained in Chapter 10, "Keeping It Fresh," expanding your contact points enhances communication, mitigates risks, and facilitates a smoother information flow.

A combination of both types of approach is needed, as well as the development of relationships beyond the main contact in the customer company.

Customer engagement refers to the extent of customer involvement in the production or delivery of the services they are acquiring. This involvement will significantly impact the overall relationship. In the case of key accounts, the level of their engagement depends on the industry and the offering that is provided. Take, for instance, the scenario of a substantial software system that is often customized to meet the customer's needs. Conversely, when dealing with many industrial components, the design and technical specifications are standardized and the supplier is guiding the customer to choose the right standard components for their need. In both cases the customer will often be cautious not to overadapt to a single supplier.

If you are working in a field where there is little customer engagement, it is possible to identify alternative engagement avenues unrelated to the core offering. One illustrative instance is the involvement in altruistic activities. Consider the American Express Members Project, an initiative where American Express allocates considerable funds to projects chosen by customers. This not only connects with customers but also creates an opportunity for interaction that fosters trust, as it demonstrates the company's genuine concern for their specific interests.[1]

---

[1] D.S. Vivek, S. Beatty, and R.M. Morgan. April 2012. "Customer Engagement: Exploring Customer Relationships Beyond Purchase." *The Journal of Marketing Theory and Practice*.

Contact With Broader Groups

Knowing where you stand within certain groups of the customer company is critical. Starting with the procurement team, followed by production, marketing, quality, legal, finance, IT, and so on, work to get a good relationship with these groups to provide a solid foundation.

Different parts of the customer company will have a different perception of you and your company, which will vary over time as well. Several of the stakeholders will be invisible, people whom you never meet but play a strong role. A vice president of procurement with one of my customers refused to meet suppliers and delegated all supplier interactions to his team. There are usually several key players who are too far from the official procurement space but still play a strong informal role. They include technology teams, plant managers, and quality experts, among others. So, your relationship building needs to be broad and sensitive to organizational changes.[2]

The state of these relationships ranges broadly between departments and individuals, as for any interpersonal relationships. You could have a healthy personal relationship with your procurement contact, a great connection with product management, a cooler relationship with the production plant, where they prefer their local supplier over your company, and a tense relationship with the legal team, which is negotiating an old claim involving your company.

Ensure there are interactions with the whole group of the decision makers or contacts so that the dynamics are understood and the relationships are broader than just with the official representatives. If the interaction you have with the customer is mainly digital, sensing these subtle positions will be difficult but not impossible. So look out for signals, and how they form a pattern over time.

Goodwill

Companies don't have memory; only people have memory. Still, a concept of corporate memory does exist; it is the know-how passed between

---

[2] B. Shankar. 2018. *Nuanced Account Management* (London: Palgrave Macmillan), pp. 57–60.

employees.[3] It is the mechanism that retains information that can't readily be stored on a computer file. Reputation is this kind of information. If your company has a good reputation, the word will spread and linger even after those involved in creating the good reputation have left their roles. The same is true for a bad reputation. Consciously build goodwill and maintain the good quality of the relationship.

For goodwill to form, work has to be done by engaging with a multitude of stakeholders in the customer company, as described in the preceding chapter. From a career perspective, a fading customer relationship is serious and it will take hard work to avoid having at least some of the blame put on you if an important client is lost.

Stockholm Syndrome

Stockholm syndrome, a condition affecting kidnapping victims who become emotionally attached to their abusers, is named after a 1973 kidnapping case in Stockholm.[4] In a broader context, you can form ties with someone who is not on your side. If you delve too deeply into the relationship between you and your procurement contact, you risk losing track of where you stand.

Balancing the three parties—you, the company you work for, and the customer—is therefore a must. When your employer, the supplier, hires you to represent another party, the customer, you need to ensure that your own integrity and values are not compromised.

If your focus is only on yourself, the customer and your company will suffer. An equal balance between all three means that none of the parties is fully served. There will be no ideal solution, as it will depend on each individual case and each individual customer. Some customers will not need a very close relationship, while others will.

Taking yourself into consideration in the calculation is important to avoid issues in the long term and feeling that you sold yourself out in favor of the customer and your employer.

---

[3] J.P. Walsh and G.R. Ungson. January 1991. *Organizational Memory*.
[4] L. Lambert. 2023. "Stockholm Syndrome," *Britannica*. www.britannica.com/science/Stockholm-syndrome (accessed January 5, 2023).

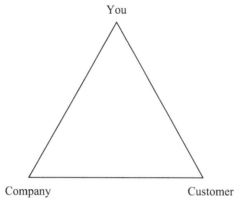

Figure 2.1 Balancing your efforts between the customer, the company you work for, and yourself requires hard trade-offs

Communicate With Confidence

Constant change is the nature of our working lives. Companies make changes on a daily basis: corporate strategy changes, discontinuing product lines, manufacturing shutdowns, entering new markets, and so on. These changes will affect your customers, and you will need to explain them. While most of these changes will not affect contracts or legal obligations, they will have an impact on the customer.

Communicating might be frustrating, for example, explaining decisions you might not have been involved in and might not even agree with. Not surprisingly, communicating uncomfortable news is often procrastinated.

The most common mistakes in communicating are:

- *Withholding information*: The KA manager doesn't convey news or decisions in a timely manner, or even at all, in order to shield the customer from unwanted information and to avoid being the messenger of bad news.
- *Detachment*: The KA manager adopts a hands-off approach, meaning the information is transferred to the customer without an attempt to save the situation.
- *Taking it personally*: When the KA manager carries more responsibility than warranted for a negative event or news, the customer may regard the KA manager as part of the problem.

The right way is simple: Communicate the news straight away, without being apologetic. If the news is really bad, you will learn how to convey it in the next chapter, "Panic Mode."

Relationships evolve, and it is easy to become blind to the changing environment. Take care to check the pulse regularly. The best way to do this is to have regular, formal reviews (most procurement teams do them anyways; if not, introduce them) to ensure the communication channel is free and clear before the relationship starts to deteriorate. That way, you have heads-up on disasters. And even when disaster strikes, there are ways to gain back customers, but it is much harder than keeping a current one.

Saving a lost customer in the SaaS business was what I was asked to do when I joined my company. I knew the customer from my past job, so I was specifically hired with this task in mind. They had terminated the contract and moved to a competitor of ours, for whom this customer was as big a fish as they were for us. I set off for the journey, re-establishing trust, conveying the benefits to the stakeholders, and supporting them off the record with business issues and questions. I sent them news, analysis, and industry rumors regularly.

Still, they were not interested, and it took me nine months to sign a minor, one-year, deal for a specific business segment. Despite the work, there were some stakeholders in one of their local business units who did not appreciate this deal and sabotaged it by deleting critical user data—we lost the contract and were delegated to the lowest supplier status.

This meant another 12 months of work to repair the relationships that still were sour when we finally could sign a more strategic partnership. So I spent two years of effort smooching and picking up the broken pieces from the breakup and putting it all back together again.

Summary

The relationship a KA manager has with the customer is close, so care is needed to not overly rely on just the personal relationship with the buyer. Doing this might lead to a one-dimensional role and will hamper the growth and development of both the account and the career of the KA manager. Combining a strong interpersonal relationship with more strategic tools, such as using analytics and processes, is a valuable step toward a mature customer relationship.

The focus of a relationship with a KA is long term, built on stability and goodwill. Maintaining a broad network of contacts within the customer company is critical, understanding that different stakeholders and departments have varying perceptions of you and your company. This opens a new dimension to interacting, complementing the strong relationship with the buyer.

A delicate balance must be maintained between the interests of the customer, your employer, and yourself to ensure integrity and value alignment. Misalignment in this trinity will cause issues, one of which is when the KA manager becomes too attached to the customer and loses sight of what the job ultimately is. This is related to the Stockholm syndrome; where hostages in a kidnapping situation became attached to the kidnapper. In business, this is akin to succumbing completely to the customer.

Confident communication, especially in challenging situations, is essential to keep the relationship healthy and transparent. Withholding information or thinking short term will backfire. Regular formal reviews can help monitor the relationship's pulse and address issues before they escalate into larger problems. Recovering a lost customer can be a challenging process that requires time, effort, and trust rebuilding after a business relationship has suffered.

CHAPTER 3

Panic Mode

Overview

- Unplanned and urgent customer incidents are daily occurrences, and though they come unexpectedly and each one is different from the others, the KA manager can be prepared for how to tackle them.
- When facing difficult situations, you must prepare for the discussion and be sure that you know what is going on and to time things correctly.
- Delivering the message requires sticking to the point and, at the same time, being humble and open to feedback from the customer. It is easy to get diverted and lose control of the conversation.
- When a solution is found, it is important to still keep on top of the issue, ensuring that the problem is suppressed for good.

A Rough Wake Up

Scenario: You get a call from a customer early one morning. An urgent shipment that was supposed to have arrived the previous night has not been dispatched from the plant. When you try to find out what went wrong, you only get some vague excuse from the back office lead who was handling the supply. The lead tries to brush it off with excuses, such as someone was absent or someone may have misunderstood the urgency. Such excuses are not exactly a force majeure that can be blamed on external factors. And you know that the impact on the customer will be massive. They relied on having the

(*Continues*)

(Continued)

> components arrive on time for trials on their assembly line, where a large gathering of their experts and other suppliers of the hardware were waiting to evaluate and fine-tune the process.
>
> You are now facing the unenviable task of informing the customer of the reason for the shipment failure. And you know the reception will be brutal. The customer will likely contact the leadership at your company and demand immediate action. It goes through your mind that you should have triple-checked the shipment schedule the previous week when there was still time.
>
> So you take a deep breath and walk slowly to the coffee machine to gather your thoughts before you make the call.

This kind of situation is what makes or breaks a KA manager: no easy solutions, and no process or support to fall back on. Seems bleak, but in reality, it's one of the main reasons your role is so important. You can compare the KA manager's job to that of an airplane pilot: Most of the time, the autopilot will fly the plane. Only in rare situations must the coolness and strong leadership of the pilot come into play. But when it does, the pilot better be up to the challenge.

Situations that are unexpected, are urgent, and have a potentially high impact will require a skilled pilot. The most common crises happen with quality, delivery, or market issues. In addition to the operational resolution of the issue, clear communications are fundamental to minimize any negative perception of the KA manager and supplier company. Communication is often the responsibility of the KA manager and, as good practice, the KA manager should be involved in deciding the solution.

The focus here is on communication you, as the KA manager, can influence. You can take the script from crisis management communications and adapt it to your environment.

Preparation

Not all situations are doomed, so in many cases, an alternative can be found that smoothly resolves the situation without any impact on the customer. If this is likely, and you need some time to develop solutions, then there is a benefit of sharing the issue with the customer immediately. It would make sense to take time to explore the situation first. When you choose to delay a response, the key question to ask is: Am I using this delay wisely? Am I using the time to my advantage by getting more information, reducing uncertainty, and initiating work on potential solutions? And are the benefits of not sharing the news straight away outweighing the drawbacks? Still, in most cases, communicating issues immediately is the best path, so the customer gets the bad news as soon as possible.

Start with understanding the situation well enough to give an explanation and answer questions with confidence. Telling a convincing story will help your counterpart have a better understanding of the situation, which should also make them more empathetic. This is even if there is no resolution proposed for the moment.

With insight into what happened and what is at stake, ask yourself if there is another way out. The more complex the company's business and situation are, the more likely something can be done to find a solution or mitigate the impact. Frequently, this requires extra costs or resources that aren't evident at first sight, but with effort, something good can come about.

> *Splashing out on a key account that matters*: During the summer months in Europe, manufacturing plants are low on staff due to vacations. If issues with quality or production output arise during these vacation months, they can cause a supply shortage—a common scenario. In one such case, it happened to the number one customer of the company. There seemed to be no solution possible, but the company's management understood the status of the customer and decided to do something that would leave a mark. They arranged to fly in plant staff from another country, which was more flexible on holidays and working hours, to boost the team at the plant that was short-staffed. This team provided extra manpower, solving the product shortage and leaving the customer very satisfied.

Often, a potential solution can be in the hands of the customer. The customer might agree to a substitute product or a trade-off such as tolerating a slight delay or accepting a compromise on quantity.

Taking the proper time to review all the information before making a decision is crucial. The eventual solution might require buy-in from your internal stakeholders, so it's better to have a solid proposal than to be forced to backtrack and change course later. Every hour or day of lost time might add up to considerable cost.

Communicating a consistent message to the customer on what happened, what was done to solve the problem, and what will be done next is absolutely crucial for the credibility of the proposal.

Getting the Message Through

When the situation is clear, what remains is to ensure that the message is transmitted to all parties involved. Despite the effort put into analysis and in finding a solution, changes can happen and new solutions will have to be found. Keep in mind when making promises that there are risks and forces beyond your control.

Lack of information allows all kinds of speculation and blame to emerge. This is avoided with comprehensive explanations of the adverse event and the efforts to mitigate it.

You can deliver the message through any one of a range of media. The rule of thumb is that the more serious the situation, the more personal the communication. However, the requirement of a quick response trumps rule number one. It is better to send a text confirming that a problem has arisen and calling or having a face-to-face meeting as soon as possible after texting than waiting for the perfect moment to have a call or meeting.

Be Proactive and Open to Feedback

When you take a strong lead by proactively stating a path of action and convincingly guiding the situation, the issues of doubt and mistrust are nipped in the bud. You get a boost of credibility if you can answer the customer's questions, debunk rumors, and evaluate the customer's counter proposals.

State it clearly if the customer has to make a decision or take action, and set a deadline for them. For example, a graphics design team that isn't able to fulfill two projects at the same time can let the customer decide which one to prioritize. They then set the deadline for the customer's decision, where delaying the decision beyond the set date will result in no work getting done.

Learn from good communicators how to answer and manage difficult situations. The conversation part is crucial as this gives the counterpart the opportunity to be part of the solution. Listening will help diffuse the situation and humility is beneficial.

Clear language is advantageous. Some corporate cultures are very direct while others less so. Adjust to your audience but be open and frank. When engaging with your customer, you are speaking with people whom you likely know well and will work with in the future. The message needs to be in harmony with your usual style of communications and reflect the severity of the situation.

In one of the overseas production locations of the company, which serves the nearby customer's assembly plant for their final products, communication was notoriously bad. This specific part of the business was new; the KA manager had been able to expand the business with this customer to new geographical areas. The plant team was used to smaller local customers, who were mostly distributors, and had a culture of not communicating delays or problems. This had not been a problem for the majority of their accounts; delays were not considered such a severe event. For the multinational customer, who globally was one of the top three accounts and had a KA status, this was major. When delivery was continuously postponed due to quality issues, the production plant didn't take much notice. Furthermore, they failed to communicate the situation clearly to the new customer, who quickly became so upset that they wanted to terminate the new contract on the grounds of gross negligence without resolution.

The message sent by the plant hadn't reflected the urgency or the severity of the situation, nor had any attempt been made to find a remedy for the situation. Had the communications been better, the customer would have understood the situation and its complex nature and might have been able to help find a solution. And this would have been done without lawyers involved.

Stick to the Script

Politicians and public relations professionals use a script to communicate during crises. They stick to the prepared story and avoid getting caught overpromising or disclosing information that doesn't help the situation. Getting off script does not end well.

A communications instructor once used this metaphor: You have three stones that represent your prepared answers. You throw one stone every time you get a question, choosing the most suitable stone for the answer but not inventing new answers. This translates to keeping to three points that you repeat to your counterpart. For example:

1. "The goods are irreparably damaged and fail to meet safety and quality standards required for use in your assembly."
2. "We can provide a smaller batch now and the remainder in three weeks' time. There is no option to deliver everything now."
3. "We will compensate for the loss according to the contract, which includes a specific paragraph addressing this type of situation. However, at this point, we have not calculated this figure, so I will come back to it when it's ready."

Deviating from this, for example, to start speculating on the monetary value of compensation, will not benefit the situation for now. Better to leave it and avoid getting caught in speculation. Done properly, it gives you the credibility and confidence to move forward as you see fit.

Resolution

With the message conveyed, and the immediate damage control done, the issue will likely remain in the spotlight for a while. Proper follow-up is crucial while continuing to provide updates of the situation to the customer.

In the best of cases, the situation will dissolve. If the correct actions were chosen, then both the technical issue and the subsequent tension should ease.

But there is a possibility that the situation will not resolve that easily, requiring active management to rectify whatever went wrong in the first attempt. Again, the same process applies: Repeat the steps and tackle the new issues. With every relapse, the relationship is tested and credibility dips. Every now and then, we face situations where things fall apart, one after the other, in very unfortunate ways. Maintaining progress is best done while keeping cool and professional.

Eventually, the issues will be resolved. When they are, the often neglected part of repairing the situation should be done: With the issue fresh in mind, do a debrief. This can be a short recap of the full situation with the customer, the management team, co-workers, service providers—all the stakeholders involved: What happened, what went wrong, and how it was resolved with an emphasis on the last part, and on any positive actions that were taken. The focus on the good work done will leave a positive view of the event and give credit where credit is due.

Anything learned and the corrective actions taken are also best shared. Often, this debrief is demanded by customers, but don't wait for that. Be proactive so that your company has a healthy feedback loop for continuous improvements, and you have the courage to evaluate your own performance.

Note, though, that the corrective actions have to be genuine and result in lasting changes.

In real life, with complex issues such as the capacity allocation, it is extremely difficult for KA managers to directly impose changes on the company they work for. In general, matrix organizations[1] cause conflicts of interest. More supervision and control will not solve these conflicts completely.

Despite this gloomy assessment, you have a lot of power to change these situations for the better. So, let's look at how to manage matrix

---

[1] A matrix organization in the corporate context is an addition to a functional chain of command, with multiple managerial accountability and responsibility functions. See L. Stuckenbruck. n.d. "The Matrix Organization," *Project Management Quarterly* 10, no. 3, pp. 21–33, accessible at PMI. www.pmi.org/

organizations and make the most of the limited resources available to KA managers.

Summary

The KA manager has a challenging role, often facing situations with no easy solutions nor lacking established processes and support to fall back on. However, this is precisely why the role is crucial and impactful. Similar to airplane pilots, KA managers can often rely on autopilot-like situations, but in crisis scenarios, their strong leadership and experience become essential.

Crises with key accounts involve unexpected, urgent, and high-impact events, often related to quality, delivery, or market issues. Handling such crises effectively requires care.

First, prepare by understanding the situation. Most often, the issues are complex; otherwise, they would not have escalated and landed on your desk, and contain many potential solutions but not a single good one. Exploring all the alternative solutions is crucial, and sometimes, the customer might have a part to play in finding the best outcome. Then, engage with the customer to start to manage the situation.

In crisis communication, it's crucial to be consistent and show leadership to navigate through the mess. Being open to the view of the customer and having a dialogue will be beneficial.

Follow-up and resolution management are the last steps to prevent any relapse of the issues that may arise after the initial response. Debriefing and sharing lessons learned from the crisis help in both solving the root causes of the issue and learning from mistakes.

Overall, KA managers play a vital role in crisis management and maintaining strong customer relationships, making their role indispensable in ensuring business success.

CHAPTER 4

Limited Resources

Overview

- Managing indirect resources and how to rely on a broad toolbox to get the most support for your customers.
- There is competition for resources not only from other customers but also from other internal initiatives and departments. The valuable stuff the company possesses is limited and everybody wants a part of it.
- Most KA managers work in companies that have a matrix design. This means building personal relationships and increasing soft power are the only way to get things done.
- Without direct authority over teams, the KA manager has to orchestrate others indirectly. General McChrystal has plenty to teach on this front.

Scraping By

A very successful KA manager told me once when we discussed the challenges of the job:

> To be honest—I always get something; I never accept that I don't get anything of what I asked for... No is not an answer, as I will threaten the management team that we will lose revenue. Every single time they succumb to my request somehow. Yes, it might be less than I was asking, but I will get sufficient support to keep the customer satisfied. So, I regularly hold my employer hostage.

The afore-mentioned case is of a very influential KA manager with a solid career, showing one way of managing limited resources. There are other ways to get support for your ideas, all of which involve influencing people with convincing arguments and communication skills.

The *Cambridge Dictionary* defines a resource as "a useful or valuable possession or quality of a country, organization, or person."[1]

Resources are valuable and, when used correctly, are the strongest possible competitive advantage that a company can have. Managing resource allocation and building and developing more resources are what strong companies do well. Hiring motivated and talented people who strive to do their best work is a significant part of a strong company's resource know-how.

The four types of resource are as follows:

- *Physical*: buildings, equipment, manufacturing plants, ...
- *Human*: employees, contractors, ...
- *Intellectual*: IP, brand, contracts, ...
- *Financial*: cash, credit lines, financial ratings, stock option plans, ...

A company's best resources are in high demand. Much of what a key customer needs, such as production capacity, R&D project teams, process development experts, technical experts, and IT systems, is not directly managed by a KA manager. This is natural; it would be unreasonable to expect that the whole organization revolved around the KA manager.

A headache for a KA manager: A large key customer's VP of procurement approaches you to suggest exploring a joint, strategic project in the field of sustainability and CO_2 reductions. Your company is an important supplier and impacts the carbon footprint of the final product. Because this is a strategic pillar for the customer, expectations are high that your company fully support the project. You can't back it half-heartedly. You must ensure success as, without the information about your products, the final product's footprint can't be calculated accurately. The underlying message is that this should be a top priority for your company.

---

[1] Cambridge Dictionary, s.v. n.d. "Resource." https://dictionary.cambridge.org/

You quickly realize that this will be a challenge. The company is working on the carbon footprint with a different methodology and this is still work in progress. You will need to get the team working on this to prepare this specifically for this client, and this will take time off their primary project. In addition, you will face the compliance and communications teams to get their buy-in. This would be needed even if the project were not to progress beyond the drawing table.

In the past, similar projects have resurfaced every now and then, with very few having real impact on the business. In the end, the pricing criteria for the customers always trumped their decisions for choosing products or suppliers based on other criteria. Your company therefore sees most of the collaborations on past projects, such as supply chain, financing, and sustainability, as wasted efforts.

How do you proceed? Upset the customer by declining the initiative, or face the internal uphill battle? Or, maybe, give it a half-hearted effort, which will slightly upset all involved but not be a major conflict for anyone?

Dilemmas like this are common, causing tension in the supplier company because allocating, to the new project, precious resources currently shared among other customers is seen as a zero-sum game.

The good news is that there is a lot you can actually do to manage situations like this and create value for your customers. This includes managing the short-term crises while steadily developing durable changes that will reduce future resource allocation conflicts.

Getting staff and experts from other departments within your company to give you their time is a critical aspect of KAM, but often, resource challenges involve trial time on production lines, access to testing, and funds for projects.

Gartner conducted a study in 2022 interviewing 372 KA managers on collaboration and efficiency of department design. Of the respondents, 76 percent answered the question "When securing resources from cross-functional colleagues, I rely primarily on…," by saying personal relationships rather than formal authority or structures.[2] Soft power is

---

[2] Gartner. 2021. *(Rebuilding) Key Account Programs for Growth*, p. 8.

a core requirement of a KA manager as it will play out on a daily basis. And the reality is that, despite efforts by the KA manager to establish operating procedures, they will only go so far in facilitating support and resources.

The Real Competition

How much more could you accomplish if you had the right resources? You feel you are allocated less than your fair share, which is extremely frustrating when you have a loyal customer who provides a reliable revenue stream to the business and clearly merits priority.

However, from the perspective of management, juggling resources is one of the most important challenges. The cold truth is that, in many cases, the overall business will not be impacted if some of the resources are withheld from key accounts. Your accounts will likely continue to purchase from you, at least in the short term.

The company might get by with giving a key customer a little bit extra, some of the time, but funding for other customers, including potential new accounts, other more profitable accounts, and all kinds of emergencies, makes it an easy decision to cut back on a key account if something else is considered more critical, as it often is. Gaining new business is much juicier than maintaining existing business.

The KA leader responded confidently when asked about the essence of KAM:

> I think a core of KAM is how an organization will enable a disproportionate resource allocation to the KA teams without damaging the morale and effectiveness of the overall company. Many companies struggle between a token claim that key customers are prioritized when they are not and squandering resources on a random selection of customers without any thought of payback. I believe the success of a KAM program depends on this. If not in tune, then the restructuring hammer will soon hit.

The time horizon plays an important role, balancing short-term results with future business success and profits. Investing in key accounts might not show any growth in the financial reports until the unfortunate day when the customer decides to leave. Then, any long-term underfunding issue becomes urgent. Still, for the overall commercial portfolio, the calculated risk of losing a customer might be outweighed by winning a new one.

Looking at the issue from this perspective, resource allocation makes sense. Individual account managers who are tireless champions for their own customers will always find it hard to accept this. The bottom line is that management counts on the KA managers to be champions of their individual customers and show loyalty to each of them while *letting the big decisions be made by the management.*

The Key Account Matrix

Mary Jo Hatch, professor in organization theory, says it well: "A major drawback of multinational corporations organized into global matrices is their often mind-boggling complexity, which demands attention to the now-three dimensions of operating this matrix: region, product, and function."[3] The KA manager knows this firsthand: Trying to get anything done in this kind of environment is like finding a way through a maze. Usually, the KAM group is part of the sales department and, then depending on the design of the matrix, two more management hierarchies based on product, geography, or project.

In this kind of fuzzy matrix world, the linear way of working with a single point of contact, engaging through the procurement counterpart, becomes tedious. Orchestrating others through soft power without direct influence is different.

The importance of the KAM function within the total business will depend on the business and company. Sometimes, the function is strategically irrelevant; other times, the key accounts play a central role in the customer portfolio, as in service industries with high added value and a great deal of reliance on a few customers. In these cases, managing the precious few clients is extremely important to the overall business.

---

[3] M.J. Hatch. 2018. *Organizational Theory* (New York, NY: Oxford University Press), p. 125.

The customers have high expectations of the KA manager. Their rosy and unrealistic view is that the supplier organization can be orchestrated effortlessly, with appropriate, informed, and motivated resources that are delivered on demand. This is, of course, not happening, as managing a matrix organization, even in the best of cases, is like herding cats.

The best way for a KA manager to navigate in a matrix organization is to focus on three functions that can be influenced and improved: managing procedures, creating personal relationships, and building winning teams.

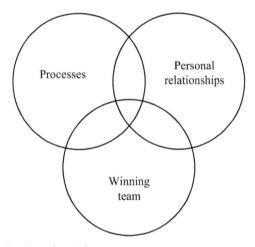

Figure 4.1 Finding the right mix

A Little Bit of Formality, Please

Ideally, you should get the other departments to play a real role in your customers' success. Sharing and mutually agreed responsibilities are massive boosters of collaboration. Many companies emphasize the customer as their first priority, but disappointingly few make this a formal objective for staff outside sales. The ideal would be co-setting goals for the matrix teams and helping the teams achieve them.

Such goals could be creating operational procedures, processes, and semiformal agreements, maybe simple agreements that can work well in companies with a casual culture.

There are circumstances where implementing formality makes sense, especially in organizations that are transitioning toward a bureaucratic management style. Here, you will have a window of opportunity for different departments and individuals to find new ways of working together. Assigning ownership to workflows is important. With the change of approach, likely with a change of management, the opportunity arises to establish a formal structure for work that was previously done by rote.

Build Personal Relationships

Smile. A simple way to make a good impression. People who smile tend to manage, teach and sell more effectively.

—Dale Carnegie

The success of Dale Carnegie's classic book *How to Win Friends and Influence People* proves that the topic has remained as valid now as it was during the 1930s. The 20 evergreen principles that he described are spot on for building strong relationships with customers.[4]

The tools for building personal relationships described in Chapter 2, "The Relationship Trap," which focuses on influencing the customer, are also valid when working with colleagues. The same can be done with the teams within your company, in order to facilitate and improve collaboration. This might not increase the pool of resources, but it will make the work more efficient.

Having team members who are not customer-facing improve their interpersonal skills by interacting with the customers will in many cases also be beneficial for their career progression.

Create a Winning Team

To be portrayed onscreen by Brad Pitt would be an honor to most of us, and General McChrystal is one of the few who has had this honor. However, this honor comes with a caveat; the film *War Machine* where Brad portrays General McChrystal is a satire of the military campaign that he led, maybe not the most flattering way of being immortalized in

---

[4] D. Carnegie. 2009. *How to Win Friends and Influence People* (New York, NY: Simon & Schuster), pp. 118–119.

film history. There is plenty of bad reputation surrounding the campaign the film is about, and indeed McChrystal resigned from the military due to some of events that happened during the campaign. But don't let that stop us from learning from his experience leading Special Forces.

During the first years of the Iraq conflict, the U.S. military's approach was built on a military dogma of centralized and efficient operations. It was a bureaucracy with a clear division of labor, rigid operating procedures, and, above all, hierarchies that dictated decision making. This environment is similar to a multinational corporation, where the KA manager is the only contact point with key customers. This way of working relies on the KA manager discussing with the procurement counterpart, taking the output from the meeting, and sharing it selectively with internal colleagues to distribute tasks. Possibly, the KA manager has to go through one or two management layers to get the approval even for small decisions. The colleagues then work independently on their respective tasks and projects and, when finished, deliver the output back to the KA manager who then, possibly adding some further processing, forwards the work to the customer—a slow and linear system, where the control and responsibility lies with the KA manager. It is a system that eliminates creativity.

This way of working, controlled and careful, has its limitations if you want to be a rock star. McChrystal introduced three ideas to make the organization more dynamic. Each of these concepts is easily applicable to KAM:

1. Sharing information freely so all members of the organization can make informed decisions. More trust was given regarding classified information so that all teams had the necessary information.
2. Decentralizing decision making. In Iraq, this translated to analysts and special operations teams collaborating and agreeing on the optimal course of action. They could engage in discussions and reach agreements without the necessity of escalating matters to higher levels of authority. This aspect is interconnected with the first point, as effective decision making relies on the availability of pertinent information.
3. Establishing regular meetings to disseminate information in a digestible form—particularly, a daily videoconference with over a hundred participants from various functions, civilians and military,

in different geographies. This allowed the large organization to be up-to-date and act as one team. A note on this last point: In 2006, a massive videoconference was probably innovative and solved issues. In today's world, when most of the time of corporate warriors is spent on video calls, introducing a conference call with dozens of participants would be outdated.[5] However, there are many ways to accomplish the task of ensuring that the stakeholders not only have access to information but also have internalized it sufficiently. They can only contribute efficiently as a group when their perception of the situation is accurate.

Be a leader and transform your lonely key account job into a team effort. Some companies actively, through operating procedures, key process indicators (KPIs), habits, and leadership, build a cross-organizational team to face the customer and jointly work for the success of the account.

Independent of how the company chooses to manage the account interaction, it is in the best interest of a KA manager to pursue a broader engagement with the customer.

Throughout this book, there is a recurrent theme of the KA manager as a lone wolf, while at the same time being part of a larger team acting like a team leader to get colleagues in a matrix organization to collaborate toward the customer's best. This seemingly contradictory position, lone wolf in a team, is embedded in the role: relentlessly leading by example and building a team while coping with the individual responsibilities.

In KAM, the lowest-hanging fruit is sharing successes and visibility with your broader team. Making all team members customer champions will likely give them an edge over their peers and kudos from the top management. This visibility costs you nothing. Since it's your job to connect with customers, you will automatically be given the credit for success, be it a project done well or a contract signed. But your supporters deserve to be put on a pedestal as much as you do.

---

[5] S. McChrystal, T. Collins, D. Silverman, and C. Fusell. 2015. *Team of Teams, New Rules for Engagement for a Complex World* (Portfolio/Penguin).

Letting them in on successes and into the magic world of customer insight gives them credibility to drive their agenda and should, ultimately, resonate with the needs of the market and those who pay their salary.

A large customer moved to e-invoicing and communicated to all suppliers the need to start implementing the new process. On the surface, there is no real possibility of gaining glory by executing a project like this. And because people dislike change, projects like this are not the most popular to work on. As the leader of the project, the KA manager took care to ensure that the new process worked well and actively promoted its success throughout the company. Buzz-words such as *digital, transformation, change, customer intimacy,* and *success* created positive visibility for everyone involved.

By sharing with the team the low-hanging fruit of success and visibility, the KA manager added a bit more credibility to the work of the team, showed the team a more beneficial way of working, and brought them their own kudos, visible to the entire company and beyond. Make this a habit that shows your team members, and potential team members, that they too can reap the benefits of suc-cess by being on your team.

Steering and shaping a matrix organization requires a lot of skill, and a lot of sweat, on the KA manager's part. Add to that customer dynamics, the challenges of dual loyalties, communications, and conflict manage-ment, and you have a recipe for stress. The next chapter will offer advice on dealing with that.

Summary

Resources, such as physical, human, intellectual, and financial assets, are true treasures and a potent competitive advantage for companies. Strong companies excel in managing these resources and in allocating them effectively.

As a KA manager, you obviously want to gain access to the resources in order to serve your customers. But these resources are often controlled by others. For example, trials on production lines, access to testing, and funds for new projects are examples of resource challenges where you might not have formal authority to decide what to do. To navigate these situations, KA managers have to rely on personal relationships, process management, and creating winning teams.

Key customers expect dedicated and immediate support, which leads to tensions between the KA manager, who conveys the customer needs to the organization, and colleagues who have other priorities.

Creating operating procedures that involve other departments implies shared responsibilities and overtly involving others in customer success. The likelihood of success will depend on the organization and corporate culture. According to research done by Gartner on the perception of KAM, personal relationships are the default way of managing KA resources.

Overall, navigating resource challenges and shaping a matrix organization require skill, dedication, and the ability to manage complexity.

CHAPTER 5

The Art of Balancing

Overview

- There is a strange duality to being a KA manager, hired by a company to represent customers. This makes the role different from many other jobs, having two opposing masters.
- Every single company has a unique culture, shaped by the environment it operates in and the kind of people it attracts. This forms the corporate culture, which influences every aspect of the work.
- Everybody has their priorities, and there will be suspicion of yours. So best to be clear about what you stand for.
- The job causes stress, and it's lonely to stand in the middle between your company and the customer. Managing this stress is a must for a long, healthy career.

When the Truth Hits

A moment of truth hits new KA managers when they realize they are hired with the task of representing another company (their customer) *and* the company that hired them. The company hired you because the voices of these customers are important enough to pay someone to represent them.

Apart from sales and customer service, other departments in your company don't experience the challenges the KA manager's dual role creates. And in many cases, even your colleagues in the sales department operate in a different world, one with much fewer intimate customer relationships.

Mastering this peculiar mindset of accommodating two different masters is fundamental to succeeding in the KA manager's job. When this balance of a dual mindset isn't dialed in correctly, you will see mismanagement:

1. *All loyalty is with the employer.* If a KA manager forgets the crucial point that the customer should come first, at first they might feel comfortable by cocooning with their colleagues but that will not last long. It will come at a significant cost. In the long term, they will lose the trust of their customers, who are likely to win in the long term, either by terminating business or by transforming the relationship into a purely transactional one. A relationship without trust will not last.

2. *All loyalty is with the customer.* The customer's priorities, not the priorities of your company, become the priorities of the KA manager. In this situation, the KA manager will be tempted to give in to the customer on things that aren't measured or don't directly impact operations. These could be, for example, avoiding imposing late payment penalties, offering extra options that haven't been contracted, or playing with open cards in negotiations, leading to a worse deal for the supplier. All these will start to adversely affect the bottom line, and eventually, the KA manager's career.

Balancing between these extremes, and doing so in a way that satisfies both masters, comes down to first being aware of the conflict and then separating the two voices.

Part of the KA manager's job is to capture, for the supplier, as much financial value as possible from the relationship with the customer while unlocking as much overall value as possible for the customer. The customer's counterpart, procurement, is expected to do the same for their side.

It is like having a freshly baked pie that is split between the two. The slice size can vary: One of you will get a bigger slice than the other. Anyone with siblings knows the challenge of splitting the pie into slices that all parties are happy with. A way to increase satisfaction is to bake a new pie to give both sides more.

Baking new pies is where the real value lies. There are many ways of doing this, which will be discussed later on in Chapter 7, "The Sweet Deal." But a fundamental aspect of it is being as supportive and forthcoming as possible with the customers and fiercely defending their rights and needs within your business. In the best cases, this new development will be big enough to soothe the conflicts caused by splitting the existing pie.

Ways of Working

Significant tension can come from the differences in ways of working and cultures between the supplier and the customer. Each company has a unique identity formed by its employees and the environment. Often, a supplier operates in a different industry from that of the customer. A plastic film manufacturer sells products to various vertical markets, each with completely different characteristics. The film manufacturer might supply packaging to toy manufacturers as well as to high-end cosmetics brands. These customers will have very different people working for them, and different values and challenges, requiring the supplier to make an effort to get the most out of the relationship.

Ultimately, it's all about the people who are executing the processes. And these individuals are bound by the company's modus operandi and likely have habits and personality traits that resonate with their companies. For example, a fashion design student is more likely to seek a job with a perfume company than with a plastic film producer, even if the roles are similar. The different proclivities of each company's employees result in two different corporate cultures.

Every transaction between two organizations is a real touchpoint where different cultures and ways of working meet and are therefore vulnerable to friction. Eliminating the likelihood of that friction is in large part on the shoulders of the KA manager.

The ideal case, the utopia of a commercial relationship, is that each of the customer processes is mirrored by a seamless process in the supplier company.[1] Alas, this never happens in reality. The KA manager, therefore, must manage the tensions that inevitably arise and function as a lubricant between the cogs.

---

[1] A. Bollard, E. Larrea, A. Singla, and R. Sood. March 1, 2017. "The Next-Generation Operating Model," McKinsey Digital.

Depending on how bureaucratic they are, companies can range from being hierarchic, formal organizations to being decentralized entrepreneurial firms whose operation is based on individuals and teams rather than written rules.[2]

Usually, companies that are bureaucratic also have clear division of labor that will attract and retain people who are comfortable with having things in order. These people further ingrain this way of working, as it is natural to them.

In the fast-moving semiconductor industry, the market moves quickly, and successful companies are agile and listen to the customers. Large capital investments are needed to turn out high-performing chips for the customers. When a customer request comes in, the answer needs to be quick, and the best companies have a "Yes we can" attitude. In these companies, the key accounts are influential and have a priority lane to get their suggestions and projects swiftly approved. The business environment demands agility and quick reaction times to be able to keep up with the market.

In faster-moving environments, growth businesses, or smaller entities, the need for versatility and rapid development requires a more entrepreneurial approach. Roles are fluid, and tasks managed ad hoc.

The challenge is in managing the gap in environments if the company and the customer have very different ways of working. The biggest challenge is clearly when the supplier is bigger and slower than the customer, rather than the other way around.

Different Priorities

To start with, a healthy approach is to accept that the people doing their jobs have different priorities. Many people who have jobs that are well structured prefer it that way, and people working in a fluid environment

---

[2] C. Duhigg. 2014. *The Power of Habit* (New York, NY: Random House).

prefer that type of environment. Since you can't change this, find a way to work with it or around it.

In informally organized companies, a lot of soft leadership is required to make things happen. Requests have to be managed individually, and persuasion skills will be what determine success.

A customer of mine once said that the quality of the work done by the company I worked for was like a high-end chef with a difficult personality: Sometimes, he produced the most amazing meal ever; sometimes, customers didn't get any food at all. Our main competitors were more like McDonalds: always the same low quality, but consistently delivered. This was a nudge for us to move to a more structured way of management, while keeping the quality high.

How to Say It

Interestingly, both the supplier and the customer will likely think that you, the KA manager, have the other company's interests in mind. Both will be suspicious of your agenda.

To keep this suspicion at bay, great communication skills come into play. Building on the material about communication in Chapter 3, how and when things are said make a difference. One bad move can destroy all the good work done.

1. *Be open about your interests*: Clarify often and consistently that you are a messenger, voicing the customer's request or interest and doing the same for the supplier.
2. *Stick to facts*: Even when you face resistance, you should not abandon the facts. There will be situations where the outcome of the decisions is not in your favor. How you react to this has a significant impact on your stress levels and your future credibility. A small white lie seems to be an easy way out but can prove devastating in the future.
3. *Use your knowledge*: In addition to providing facts, use your specific know-how to suggest solutions and find positive outcomes that will help your customers.
4. *Be frank, not self-incriminating*: You should strike a balance between not taking the blame personally and, at the same time, owning up to

the situation and suggesting solutions. Keep in mind how the situation will impact your integrity.

5. *Managing the fallout*: You will be affected by most business issues, be they the loss of goodwill, trust, money, or business. So, take extra care that at least goodwill and trust are kept as intact as possible.

How I said "no" to a customer: The recipient of my refusal was a prominent player in the travel sector, a renowned company that had recently been assigned to me as a key account. The move was primarily due to the potential their business could offer us and their status as a strong customer reference. Their scale versus their suppliers, most of whom were a fraction of the size, gave them unproportional power. Unfortunately, they abused this authority by being arrogant.

This approach clashed heavily with our culture. We were a small software firm known for a strong and positive work environment. The customer had a habit of tinkering with our product—a specific software that formed part of their massive IT infrastructure. Much like a carefully assembled Lego creation that we had patiently built, they came as a playground bully to mess with it until it broke. This happened over and over, and every time it broke, they called upon us to fix it. The indifference to our advice made the situation very frustrating. Even if they paid for the work, this habit became more and more of a problem, so I suggested to my leadership team that we terminate the customer relationship. The cost on our workforce, who got demotivated and were in constant firefighting mode, combined with the unbalanced and arrogant relationship, was such that we could not conduct constructive discussions about new business. Most of the time I interacted with the customer was spent on calls on how we could urgently fix what they had broken and the blame being thrown at us.

With the support of my management team, who understood the problem, I terminated the business we had with them on very good terms. We supported the new supplier by transferring know-how and I took care in maintaining a very professional relationship with all the customer stakeholders. This paid off a few years later

> when I identified a new business opportunity with this same customer, a new product group where we could add a lot of value. When approaching the customer this time, the tone was different, and the respect and basis of the relationship were different. The new business was developed better, without tinkering and problems, making them a very valuable KA.

It's Lonely at the Job

As a colleague used to say, "Be like a swan, calm above the surface, kicking frantically below." You will be the one standing alone, facing the customer, while the rest of the team looks on.

The job can get lonely when the heat is on. Raising issues will lead to potential conflicts within your company. Much of the tension is due to limited resources, which is a common occurrence in many companies.[3] Deploying just enough resources to get the job done and managing them skillfully to get the most out of them make a company efficient.

Loneliness is also caused by a corporate silo structure, emphasized by different cultures in each silo. You might have difficulties connecting with the headquarters if you are located in a distant country with a different culture or, as is often the case for larger global accounts, you sit in an ivory tower and sense the distrust of local teams who manage local accounts. Despite the best efforts to make KAM a team sport, there will be times of standing alone. For the KA manager to fit well with the customer's culture might result in disengagement with the corporate culture. A KA manager who strongly exhibits company cultural traits might alienate the customer.

Constant Stress

Pressure from work and particularly the stress the KA manager job exerts can be hard to handle. How we respond to stress is partly hardwired into our brain. We react with the same tools as we did thousands of years ago

---

[3] A. Morgan and M. Barden. 2015. *A Beautiful Constraint* (London: Wiley).

when we were in immediate physical danger. Evolution hasn't updated this functionality since then, so we are stuck with a reaction that isn't ideal for the current situation. When stress signals continue, as it is with work, for longer periods, maybe years, it becomes chronic, which is bad news; it will start to take effect on us physically. Many of the brightest rock stars burnt out early, leaving the world mourning and wondering what they could have accomplished if their careers had spanned decades instead of just a few years.

The advice for work–life balance to counter the pressure from work with more free time, and more unwinding during this time off, is only part of the solution. "The only way to get the work–life balance right is to enjoy what you do," states Carl Vernon, a renowned expert on the topic.[4] With the right approach, this stress can be turned into excitement, motivation, and drive.

All this needs to be managed, and there are plenty of tools to facilitate this:[5]

- *Off-work*: Recover well and the stress of the day won't linger and start poisoning your private life. Small doses of stress are good for us; our reactions are well suited for immediate threats and short-time pressure. But our body needs to calm down to prepare for the challenges the day after. Three main tools mitigate stress. These are the same tools that help in weight loss and provide for a longer and healthier life and overall well-being: sports and physical exercise, avoiding alcohol, and a healthy diet.

- *Work*: In the heat of the moment, there are quick tools to calm the worst pressure. Mindfulness, which is paying attention purposefully and accepting the current situation without judgment, is one of the most effective tools to avoid the brain jumping straight into fight or flight mode. Adapting your expectations and reactions to circumstances in the workplace, while taking a consciously calm approach

[4] C. Vernon. 2017. *The Less Stress Lifestyle* (UK: Headline Publishing Group), p. 39.
[5] J. Sutton. February 23, 2018. "10 Techniques to Manage Stress," Positive Psychology.

to interactions, will help. The Navy SEALs, a military special operations force, use a breathing technique to reduce stress during high-stress situations. Box breathing is simple; it takes only a few minutes, so is ideal for incorporating it into the work habits. Box breathing is a breathing cycle based on four phases, each the same length of time. Start by inhaling slowly counting to four, then hold the breath, again counting to four, exhale counting to four, and wait for four counts when the lungs are empty before starting the breathing cycle again. Do this for a few minutes and the body will get an immediate recharge and you will be ready for the next battle if you are a SEAL—or to a call to a customer if you are a KA manager.[6]

- *Longer-term, structural changes:* Finding purpose in what you do is the most solid, long-term way of turning stress into excitement. Stress and excitement are emotions that lie within the same psychological state; the key difference between the two is the presence of fear.[7] Most of us perceive excitement as positive and stress as negative. If you are in flow—a mental state where your skills match the task and you are doing what you enjoy—the body is not drained but energized. Throughout the book, I have emphasized love for the job, and the reduction of stress is only one aspect of what it brings to be truly passionate about what you do.

Stress is, largely, a result of expectations we put on ourselves: what we expect from others, and what they, in turn, expect from us. With increased awareness and emotional intelligence, stress will be easier to manage. Be aware of your emotions and how you express them to others, and have the confidence to move forward on collaborations despite pushbacks or conflicts.

---

[6] M. Greenberg. 2016. *The Stress Proof Brain* (Oakland: New Harbinger Publications, Inc).

[7] A.W. Brooks. 2013. "Get Excited: Reappraising Pre-Performance Anxiety as Excitement," *Journal of Experimental Psychology*.

Summary

The KA manager needs to strike a balance between the company they are working for and the customers they carry responsibility for. Working for the success of both is almost an impossible challenge that can only be accomplished by carefully balancing the wishes of the two masters without selling yourself out. Mismanagement occurs if loyalty is too tilted toward either side, and this inevitably will result in a loss of trust and respect.

The KA manager's role involves capturing financial value for the company while, at the same time, unlocking value for the customer. Real value is created if the KA manager accomplishes both objectives.

Each company has its ways of working and its own culture. A corporate culture attracts like-minded people and forms the identity of the company. In commercial relationships, there can be two, sometimes very different, cultures forced to collaborate and engage with each other. The melding point is the KA manager who needs to translate the separate languages of these two worlds. Communications play an important role in accomplishing this. Successfully navigating the dual role requires finesse, effective communication, and adept conflict management.

Being the point between two masses can lead to loneliness, detached from either side and pressured by both. This induces stress on the KA manager; there is often no leeway on either entity: customer or company. Saying no to the customer is often not an option; at the same time, the KA manager has no direct control of the company's resources or decisions. To have a long and healthy career, it is up to the KA manager to handle the stress.

CHAPTER 6

Sell Me This Pen

Overview

- Learn the fundamentals of sales from the Wolf of Wall Street, Jordan Belfort.
- Body language is a must in high-stakes commercial transactions; we learn from Joe Navarro on how to read people and interpret nonverbal signals.
- KA management-specific tools come in handy when pursuing new business with existing customers.

Good Old Selling

Pure, basic selling is a skill that will always be in high demand. Acquiring new clients, cold calling, managing the sales funnel, scoping the market, and so on, all play part in the life of a KA manager.

To learn hands-on sales skills, why not enlist Leonardo di Caprio as our teacher? Actually, the real character behind Leonardo's role in *The Wolf of Wall Street* is Jordan Belfort, whose story is the basis of this movie. Belfort is a sales professional and inspirational speaker. He started by selling penny stocks to naive investors, moved into various illegal transactions, and spent time in prison, but upon release, he became an engaging speaker on sales wisdom.

Jordan is of the opinion that no matter what is sold, the process is the same. In the movie, a now famous scene, dubbed "Sell Me This Pen," demonstrates the essence of this sales philosophy: Belfort challenges someone to role-play as a pen salesman. The man's task is to sell Jordan a pen that Jordan just handed to him. Simple task, but most fail at it. Why?

The core principle of Jordan's selling technique is that the potential customer has to have a genuine interest in the purchase. To spend effort on someone who is not interested in the product is a waste of time. In the "Sell Me This Pen" example, the seller must start by probing the prospective buyer's interest in, and need for, a pen.

As a KA manager, you need to understand your prospective customers' position and interest in pens. What would the prospective customers use the pen for? Do they own a pen already? Was there a time they had a problem with a pen? With such insights into what benefits they would appreciate from owning a pen, the seller can move to a sales pitch crafted for this specific prospective customer.

Listening and observing are the keys to this technique. Add awareness of both verbal and nonverbal signals, and "Sell Me This Pen" becomes a crash course in sales.

In his sales model, Jordan champions three needs that have to be right for the sale to succeed:

1. The prospective customer must need the product or service and like what you are offering.
2. The prospective customer must trust you and connect with you.
3. The prospective customer needs to trust and connect with the company you represent.

A great salesperson will work to increase the prospective customer's satisfaction so that all three of these needs are met until the customer is comfortable with making the purchase. For an existing KA customer, the first and third criteria are usually fulfilled before you step in, and the second will be up to you.

Then, to take the buying decision further, there are two different tactics:

1. *Lower the action threshold*: Avoid mental barriers that make the deal difficult. A lower action threshold can be achieved by having the product readily available, avoiding a cumbersome process for making a purchase order, making implementation easy, and removing risk as much as possible. Risk mitigation can be done through money-back

offers, trial periods, and so on, so the customer can transition easily, risk-free, into becoming a user, without having to make a much harder commitment that will be difficult to mitigate or reverse.

2. *Raise the pain threshold (of not buying)*: Highlight what is lost by not buying. The pain threshold is increased by letting prospective customers explain and reflect on the shortcomings of a different product they already possess or the disadvantages of not having any product at all. Do this without trying to diminish their feeling of pain and then tailor your product pitch to alleviate the pain.

After forming a clear understanding of your prospective customer's needs, beliefs, fears, constraints, and priorities, and estimating the financial situation, transition to your prerehearsed sales pitch. Admittedly, these factors are harder for a KA manager to influence, but there is still leeway. A skilled KA manager will subtly highlight and enforce what the buyer might already know.

Probe your customers, even if you know them and their use of the product. There will be new insights to be learned even when you think you have a solid grasp of the situation. If your company has done business with the customer for some time, a lot of intelligence is already available. And you are likely offering something much more complex than a pen, which means that there will be a large number of stakeholders in the buying process who have their own needs. This will probably require much more probing and more than one short conversation with one person. But the basics are the same.

You are not likely to make many cold calls in the KA manager role, at most a warm call with a respondent who is receptive to your message.

When the time is ripe, and you think you have a sufficient amount of insight, move to the pitch. First, pinpoint the customer's needs and then formulate a pitch that answers them and, at the same time, lowers the action threshold. The customer should already feel the pain of not buying after you have discussed the current shortcomings that the customer is experiencing. How much and what kind of pitch will depend on you and the product. In some cases, the buyer will be an expert who needs to translate your offer into a sales pitch they can use in their company, and you just need to give them a helping hand. Other times, you will need to put much more work into your pitch.

Nonverbal Communication

An old saying claims that 93 percent of all communication is nonverbal. That's not really true, but it makes a nice headline. This claim derives from studies by Albert Mehrabian in the 1960s. Recorded messages using emotionally loaded words were spoken in a tone of voice that were inconsistent with the spoken message. In addition, the messages were combined with photographs showing someone expressing yet another different emotion. A group of observers evaluated these combinations of recorded voices expressing a different emotion from the one shown in the accompanying photo. The author concluded that the visual and tonal clues were stronger than the actual words in conveying emotions. While these experiments are interesting and valid, they are not applicable as-is to the business context. In fact, the author himself stated that the results were not something that could be widely applied to any communication. In conclusion, the claim that 93 percent of communication is nonverbal is a myth that should be debunked for good.[1]

Nevertheless, the tone of voice, body language, and facial expressions are fundamental for any advanced conversation. In sales, awareness of nonverbal communication and interpretation of the counterpart's nonverbal cues make a massive difference in outcomes.

Empathy is part of any good interpretation, and there are tools that expedite people-reading and communicating efficiently. If you also have a good memory, you will bond more easily with people and gain their trust.

Expert Joe Navarro, an ex-FBI agent known as the human lie detector, has a deep understanding of people-reading.[2]

The way to do it:

1. *Be a competent observer of your environment.* Continuously read the people you engage with; observe their body language and how it changes.

---

[1] A. Mehrabian and M. Wiener. 1967. "Decoding of Inconsistent Communications," *Journal of Personality and Social Psychology* 6, pp. 109–114.

[2] J. Navarro and M. Karlins. 2009. *What Every BODY Is Saying* (New York, NY: William Morrow).

2. *Observe in context*: Is the person's reaction in line with what you expected? Someone on a first date, for example, is supposed to be a bit nervous, so that's nothing to be concerned about.

3. *Universal codes and clusters of signals*: Crossing legs and other obvious examples of body language are common across cultures. Usually, they are the quick tips that need to be learned individually, and when you are aware of them, they are easy to spot.

4. *Idiosyncratic behavior*: A change in someone's habitual behavior might mean that something is wrong. Spend face-to-face time with people, as you probably already do with your customers, and get to know the behavior of each individual.

5. *Changes in their behavior*: Learn how your counterparts behave in different environments so that you can spot deviations in specific situations, such as during negotiations when your counterpart is under pressure.

6. *Baseline behavior*: Idiosyncratic behavior provides a picture of someone's identity in normal situations. The more you know about someone's baseline behavior, the better you'll be able to filter out false signals.

7. *Multiple signals*: Mixed signals can offer more insight than just one behavior. During a negotiation, participants who exhibit stress behavior followed by pacifying behavior could be revealing that they are bargaining from a position of weakness.

8. *Be subtle when observing others*: Become a savvy spy without revealing your intention when you study the behavior of others.

Small but Essential Tools

All the normal sales advice is valid for KA managers: Increase sales, understand the customer, and be a strong negotiator. On top of this, there are some aspects of the job that are more important when dealing with long-term customers:

- *Cross-selling or upselling*: The amount (as a percentage of their needs) of goods that large customers purchase is often stable, year in and year out. The customer might have split the total supply among several suppliers, by percentages or by quantity, based on their procurement strategy and risk management. Changes in how much can be sold of these products to this particular customer is thus dependent on the success of their sales: More sales to the customer means more sales for the KA manager.

In this situation, cross-selling and upselling are a way to increase revenues and improve margins, especially when the primary products or services are subject to high cost pressure. Identifying the opportunities in other areas of the customer's business requires thinking outside the box. They may, for example, be buying financial software, and you are also offering risk management software that can fit the needs of the legal team.

For upselling, you can use the classic sales tools, and with R&D's backing, you can offer something exciting to the customer. If innovations are differentiated and solve valuable problems, then your job is easy. If the fit is not that great, which is the case for many tangible business-to-business products, then the challenge is maybe tougher and you'll need to identify the opportunities carefully.

- *Acting as a consultant*: Your role as a knowledge expert opens the door to being a (free) consultant providing insight into your customer's operations. If you show that you are bringing value to them without gaining any direct benefit for yourself, you will be perceived differently: You will become a valuable partner for the customer.

- *Knowing how to handle delays*: Often, the procurement process gets stuck at a late stage, after you have sent your offer and are waiting for a final approval or rejection. This is normal, and with your experience of the industry and specific habits of each customer, you will know what to expect. Some customers are quick and clear; others go back and forth and take plenty of time to approve a sale.

The two main reasons for any unusual delay that affords you an opportunity to take action, or at least gain insight, are (1) technical delays that you can have an influence on and (2) a serious competitive threat to the deal.

Getting more insight into the delay from your network allows you to react accordingly. If the issue is technical, be proactive. Give a helping hand and involve experts from your business if that is relevant. If you can't identify any real technical issue, a competitor could be involved in negotiations, and you are left hanging in case things don't work out with the competitor.

Always have a validity date for your offers so you are not stuck waiting and try to ensure that if the deal between the customer and your competitor doesn't work out, you have the flexibility to revise your offer.

Master the basics of sales for those crucial moments when negotiating, upselling, or just maintaining the sales will make the engagement much more solid. Some KA managers prefer the comfortable environment of the office, behind the desk, working on plans, and reviewing e-mails, rather than the harsh environment of sales. Don't fall into this habit. Rather, look actively for opportunities where the customer has a need that you can fulfill.

Once your customers are convinced that your product is exactly what they need and agree to buy it, you can embark on one of the most exciting parts of your job: negotiating.

A large part of negotiating is in:

- Preparation
- Person-to-person exchange of information
- Contract finalization

This is where the big-picture directions are set and the financial foundations are laid. Multiyear contracts require long-term views and careful consideration of what the future looks like. This is the art of the deal, which we look at in the next chapter.

Summary

This chapter highlights the enduring importance of pure, basic selling skills. While KAM is mostly about managing existing businesses, skills in how to sell are still fundamental for success in the role. Jordan Belfort, an influential figure in sales, has much to teach.

Understanding the customer's position and listening are starting points. Then there are three criteria for a favorable setup in sales: (1) the customer must need the product, or service; (2) the customer must trust you; and (3) the prospective customer needs to trust the company you represent. Without these prerequisites, closing a sale is very difficult. When a salesperson interacts with a potential customer who meets these criteria, they should emphasize the pain the customer will have if not purchasing while simultaneously reducing the barriers for the customer to commit to the deal. This then makes the customer receptive to a great, clear, and digestible sales pitch.

Nonverbal communication, as taught by Joe Navarro, holds significance during commercial negotiations and in comprehending the customer's needs and preferences. Much can be interpreted and understood from observing the counterpart while negotiating.

There are three KAM-specific sales techniques: cross-selling or upselling, consultive sales, and handling delays that frequently surface with key customers. These tools are essential to maximize the chances of success.

CHAPTER 7

The Sweet Deal

Overview

- Winning commercial deals is the lifeblood of sales, with KAM being no exception.
- Major negotiations require structure and knowledge of effective negotiation techniques.
- The special characteristics of KAM are long contracts, broad customer insight, and strong relationships that will require collaboration years after the deal is signed.

Negotiations

One of the most rewarding and visible parts of the KA manager's job is negotiating contracts. For anyone in sales, the moment of closing a deal is the ultimate goal, the winning moment. And salespeople like winning.

Closing a deal is often a long process that calls for a lot of work to be done to achieve the final climax of putting ink to paper: product development, business intelligence, strategy formulation, market research, and identification of potential customers to fulfill other aspects of the closure package.

Negotiations are a significant part of all sales relationships, and key account negotiations have some special characteristics. They are often complex, take a long time to conclude, and include points that an average sales negotiation doesn't. These are usually not directly related to the price, and include quality, finances, innovation, and complex delivery terms such as just-in-time, integrated supply chains, and risk management. For instance, stock levels is a negotiation point that play a sizable role when the agreement strongly impacts the operations of both parties. If we are speaking about multiyear contracts the demands increase exponentially. The large amount of detail that has to be worked out would not be cost-effective for a one-off transaction or a contract that would be renegotiated annually.

What exactly is a negotiation? The simplest definition of a negotiation is "a discussion to reach agreement." An elegant addition to this definition is "that is satisfying for both parties," which refers to the collaborative aspect of the negotiation:

A discussion to reach an agreement that is satisfying for both parties.

In most business cases, agreement is reached because it offers *good-enough* business for both parties. And for KAM, the need for both parties to be satisfied is critical. A bar at a remote beach can sell cold drinks on a hot day for an exorbitant price and get away with it. With a key customer, you will not live long if your counterpart thinks you are ripping them off.

Know Your Customer

In any large organization, there are multiple stakeholders, each with their own targets and priorities. This leads to complex negotiations and a lot of skill to bring maximum value from the agreement. You are expected to navigate the customer company to understand and translate their needs into a competitive offer and then negotiate successfully to win the business.

After the closing, you are obliged to do business with them within the terms of the contract, which means that short-term, unilateral wins can backfire.

An important aspect that differentiates a business-to-consumer negotiation from a business-to-business is knowing who has the best insight into the price of the goods or services under negotiation.

In a business-to-business setting, the buyer is often the one who has the most accurate information on the market price. Large businesses are often tendered, giving customers the opportunity of a tailored offer from several suppliers. The seller seldom has this detailed information, as quality specifications, delivery requirements, and other aspects of the sale will influence the offer. In addition, the customer knows best how performance and quality level will impact the final product. For example, supplying the airline industry with basic components such as screws and bolts is much more demanding and pricier than supplying similar-looking products to other industries. Certifications, quality control, higher scrap rate, traceability—all render the same bolt a completely different product in the pricing context.

The seller usually has no insight into the full impact of the procured product. The buyer knows exactly which specifications are required, how the final product will perform with a subcomponent or service, and how it will impact the end user. Often, the buyer has a better insight into the competition because the details of business-to-business contracts, specifications, terms, and prices are not publicly available. Complex proposals don't offer readily available price information as do business-to-consumer products. Only by examining several tenders with the same characteristics can prices be compared to arrive at a reasonable average, and usually only the buyer has this information.

Your procurement counterpart is an expert in the field and likely operates within a large company where various stakeholders have different expectations of quality and service levels. Frequently, the procurement team has cost as their main concern. The production team values seamless delivery and smoothly running operations. The quality team sees defect rates. The marketing team focuses on the perceived quality of the final product, and so forth—not to forget additional, intangible company requirements, such as locally sourced, sustainability, impact on working capital, risk management, and financial reliability of the supplier. Therefore, the various stakeholders will likely disagree on supplier selection, and the final winner potentially won't be the first choice of all stakeholders.

The customer usually has several alternatives for any supply source. In some businesses, choice for demanding customers might be limited due to consolidated markets or restrictive specifications. Still, it's safe to say that there will be options, and in special cases where there is only one solution, the customer's procurement team will undoubtedly develop other options, which can include another supplier's substitute product or a way to reduce reliance on suppliers where the risk is too high. Porter's five forces tool (see Chapter 1, "Know Them as You Know Yourself") indicates where such pressure comes from.

You already have an ongoing relationship with the customer and may have had it for a long time. You know your counterpart's negotiation style, strengths, and weaknesses and how the various stakeholders function.

The stakeholders in the customer's organization will influence the buyer and, as some of them will be the direct users of the product or service you are providing, their preferences guide the decision of the buyer. So it is worth considering the buyer's actions as driven by independent entities with separate requirements—and then the price component, which is the ultimate driver when all other aspects are satisfying the stakeholders.

Negotiation Process à la KAM

During the COVID-19 pandemic of 2020–2022, the EU partnered with the pharmaceutical company AstraZeneca to provide vaccines. It was done in a rush, seemingly with the best intentions of both parties. When reality hit a few months later, production issues surfaced: A massive triage emerged between the EU, the UK and AstraZeneca about who should receive the scarce vaccine doses. It ended in a lawsuit over the wording in the contract.[1] The outcome was clearly a disaster for both parties. From the KAM perspective, there is a take-away from the COVID-19 example: You should realize, from you knowledge of the business, that production capacity is limited, including ramp-up risk. But you have to deal with several powerful customers who expect priority in product delivery.

This is of course a unique case. Politics played a strong role here, with Brexit making the EU and U.K. relations "complicated" to say the least. Still, it is undeniable that unclear contractual clauses open the door to the risk of severe damage to the relationship, seriously impacting your business and your career.

---

[1] A. Isaac and J. Deutsch. February 22, 2021. "How the UK Gained an Edge With AstraZeneca's Vaccine Commitments," *Politico*.

Context

Understanding the nature of all the players at the table—company dynamics, customer–supplier history, and current business drivers—forms the context of the negotiation.

The history aspect can be significant, sometimes making the negotiation more reminiscent of marriage counseling than a business transaction. Once, I had a customer insisting on a clause that would give them the right to veto the appointment of the staff who interacted with them because of past experiences with a KA manager whom they disliked.

Preparation

Try to capture on paper all the complexity—all the figures and all the scenarios—and spin them until they make sense to you. Assumptions are acceptable, and most of the time, the 80/20 rule will suffice.

This is the time to find the best alternative in case the deal falls through: a walk-away option or best alternative to negotiated agreement (BATNA). This should be a realistic option and, however bad it is, should form the basis of your lowest acceptable offer. If this alternative looks really bad, work on having better options. The worst situation in a negotiation is assuming there is no option to an agreement, which leads to desperation to come to an agreement at all costs.

A very large and powerful customer might give the impression there are no alternatives in case an agreement cannot be found, resulting in a loss of business and downsizing of the current workforce. Hopefully, you have several BATNAs, such as serving other customers, reallocating resources, and other ways to mitigate a loss.

"There is no alternative. We have to win this deal" is a common mindset that is extremely damaging. It puts unnecessary pressure on closing a deal and hands over inordinate power to the counterpart. There is always a BATNA. It might be bad, but it exists.

Once you've settled on your BATNA, don't deviate from it in the heat of battle.

Negotiation

When it comes to the real game of negotiations, procurement has plenty of tricks up their sleeves. Knowing these tricks comes in handy, but in the end, all situations are different and will be more challenging in reality than in rehearsal. In real life, negotiators may be unprepared and disorganized. It is important that you make sure your team is prepared and team members know the role each one of them will play. It's best they play their assigned role every time they get together to discuss the negotiation, be it related to technicalities, timing, or price.

Winners' Remorse

Pricing is an activity managed surprisingly differently across companies. Some companies have a dedicated pricing function responsible for analyzing and implementing prices, while in others, a product manager sets a range and provides guidelines to sales. In many cases, the KA manager holds significant responsibility, either supported by a team or working independently, for pricing and as a consequence, for the profitability of the customer. Pricing is probably the strongest tool in the commercial toolkit. It makes or breaks a deal, it determines if the company will make money on conducting the business, and it signals what the perceived value of the full offering is to the customer. And it is only a number. Other features that have similar power are quality, product performance, and design, which all take enormous effort and time to create. Creating a price takes an instance. We all know the agony of trying to settle for a price for an important business offer—knowing that if it is just a few percentages too high, we might lose the business, but at the same time, we might be leaving a lot of money on the table if we sell too cheaply. And we very rarely will find out what the customer's walkaway price is.

Perversely, when concluding negotiations successfully, there is sometimes a feeling of defeat. Winners' remorse is when you get second thoughts about a deal, such as whether an even better deal could have been made. In reality, however, there is no perfect price; it's always either too high or too low, leading to this conundrum every single time a deal is done. Too high a price will result in the customer walking away, and too low a price means that money was left on the table.

The original winners' remorse theory is based on George Akerlof's research about assymetrical information in business transactions. This reasearch was eventually awarded a Nobel Prize in Economics in 2001.[2] The theory holds that when information about the product is not equally available to both seller and buyer, it is almost always the seller who will have more insight into the true value of the goods. The buyer who can't determine whether the food is good (peach) or bad (lemon) will always have to assume the worst. For example, with used cars, there are some good, well-maintained vehicles while others are technically faulty. Taking into consideration the variety of cars on the market, and the fact that only the sellers know the actual condition of their cars, the sellers price the car according to their perception of its value. The smart seller of a lemon will hike up the price and claim the faulty vehicle is good, a peach. Buyers realize the market is mixed with lemons and peaches and come to believe the sellers always price all their vehicles as peaches. This, in turn, leads the buyers to assume all the vehicles are lemons. The sellers of the best peaches won't get the just price and, in theory, will never sell these mint cars, breeding mistrust and distrorting the market. This scenario may be a bit overdramatic but still the logic has merit. There are many ways to protect the less informed party from the risks derriving from assymetrical information. For example, a warranty on a used car mitiagates the information assymetry and allows for the market to function.

Staying Cool

It would be foolish to claim that emotions aren't part of a negotiation. The history of the relationship between seller and buyer will flavor decisions, personal relationships can't be disregarded, and soft skills or communication will impact the outcome. These will inevitably be part of the preparation process but should be extremely well managed at the negotiating table.

---

[2] G. Akerlof 1970. "The Market for "Lemons": Quality Uncertainty and the Market Mechanism." *The Quarterly Journal of Economics* 84, no. 3, pp. 488–500.

Since it's impossible to fully suppress emotions, the supplier's KAM team should review together how to express and process their emotions to deliver their case as clearly and objectively as possible.

Follow-Through

After an agreement is reached, and the main points of the agreement are closed, the negotiations are, supposedly, over. However, there is still plenty of work to do. An integral part of the negotiation lies in recording the high-level agreement in a detailed, unambiguous, legal document that binds both parties. More often than not, this phase of the negotiation gives rise to renegotiations. In addition to the main pillars of the agreement, many aspects that were agreed on initially are often interpreted differently by the parties involved. They may contain contradictions or details that make it necessary to adjust the wording. It is often after the agreement is written, using legal terms, that these differences are noticed. Most often, only minor parts need clarification, but sometimes, major items are put on the table.

When the actual, detailed meaning has been clarified, my first piece of advice is to keep the document as simple as possible but still with just enough details to avoid misinterpretation. Leave most details in appendices and service level agreements such as product lists, location names, and the schedule for various obligations. Basically, all information that might change over time should be separated from the main contract.

When the final contract is signed, the task remains to communicate the news to the stakeholders. What you communicate depends on the context. It can be the full contract details or just some highlights that are relevant to the target audience.

Sharing gives the stakeholders insight into what is expected of them as well as others in your company. In addition, communicating contract details is a valuable tool to show leadership your professional successes and allow visibility to your work. This leads us to the broader topic of communications, which we discuss in the next chapter.

Summary

Negotiations are a highly rewarding and critical aspect of the KA manager's job. Understanding the customer, including all the stakeholders involved, remains as important during the final negotiations as during the beginning of the sales process.

The definition of a negotiation is essentially a discussion to reach a mutually satisfying agreement between parties. KA negotiations are characterized by being complex, time-consuming, and encompassing a long list of attributes beyond price, such as quality, finance, innovation, and delivery terms. Key account managers need to be well prepared before sitting down to negotiate and ensure that they know what the alternatives are to reaching an agreement with the customer. Negotiating without having a fallback option puts undue pressure on reaching an agreement. Setting clear limits of what the minimally acceptable agreement might look like takes away last-minute emotional concessions that are later regretted. With a walkway proposal in mind beforehand, there is no need to rethink what is acceptable in the heat of the moment.

In complex organizations, multiple stakeholders, some of whom are invisible and some of whom have conflicting interests, are involved in the negotiations. They will influence the outcome of the negotiations, underscoring the need for the KA manager to consider their perspective.

After reaching an agreement, proper follow-through is vital, as coming to a detailed, and legally binding, contract often requires further clarification and adjustments. The last step, skillfully communicating the agreement to everybody involved, makes fulfilling the new obligations easier.

CHAPTER 8

Keep It Simple

Overview

- The world of communications: how the different ways of communicating work, including using silence effectively.
- Stakeholders in the customer organization will assign to the KA manager a sales persona, a kind of archetype based on their limited knowledge of you as a person. This persona will affect how they perceive everything that you do.
- Keeping track of business, by using tools or an excellent memory, makes the job easier and will boost your credibility.

Communicating With Ease

Communication plays a very important role in the life of a KA manager. All forms of communication—face-to-face, improvised small talk, formal, legal documents, and everything in between—come into play. When it's about conveying difficult, complex, and delicate topics, the following components should be taken into consideration:

1. *Verbal communication*: Using precise and accurate wording is critical to ensure that all stakeholders understand the message. Knowing what not to say, the use of silence, and properly engaging in the dialogue are equally important.
2. *Written communication*: Careful structure and wording are essential to deliver a clear, unambiguous message. In addition, the communication should be attractive from a sales or marketing point of view.
3. *Orchestration*: This includes overall clarity and efficacy, which medium to use on each occasion (verbal, e-mail, conference call, etc.), how and when to schedule meetings, when to engage in group versus private conversations, and so on.

4. *Administration*: Records should be managed to avoid chaos, including the use of various customer relationship management (CRM) systems and keeping track of e-mail, correspondence, and all other documentation, such as contracts.

5. *Trust and compassion*: These emotional factors are vitally important to ensure that the whole message reaches the receiver and is accepted and believed.

6. *Awareness*: Your awareness of business priorities and their impact on both supplier and customer business helps you to choose your battles and adjust the response accordingly. A minor delay in the supplier's delivery of a minor component might have an outsized impact on the customer's final deliverable to their own customer. Understanding the situation and facts at hand will give you the necessary awareness.

Listening is the primary component of communication. Without it, you are left with a one-sided monologue. It is better for the KA manager to err on the side of too much listening rather than too little. And by *listening*, I mean fully focused listening.

In business contexts, language needs to be simple and clear. Waste no words in delivering the complete message to your counterpart. Use easily digested language.

Jargon is best avoided in written communication. In verbal conversations selective use of jargon is acceptable as you know if the receiver is familiar with the terminology and realize soon if there are terms that are not understood. Nevertheless, in verbal communication, overusing jargon gives the impression of arrogance and should be avoided, as should using too many abbreviations and acronyms. It takes a couple of seconds to spell out an abbreviation or acronym, unless it is so commonly used that everyone knows what it means.

When the basics of communication are well managed, the power of storytelling can bring a lot of life into your message. A story told in a compelling and flowing way is much better received than the same message conveyed in a data-centric way and the presenter is more highly regarded. For all interactions where a message is conveyed, move to the storytelling approach where the story is adapted to the listener.

Rehearsing the message so you speak with confidence will turbocharge your communication skills.

For those unfamiliar with storytelling, all parents will know the power of creating a powerful story. The easiest is personal anecdotes—cases where you can engage the audience when they relate to the characters in your story. Most businesses today rely on customer cases to communicate the value of their products; the more complex the product, the better. Be attentive to finding good stories; they are everywhere.

But, what if you feel that the product or service your company is offering can't be easily intertwined into a story that flows in front of customers? If there is no story to be told in front of a key account, the value proposition is probably weak. If you can't convincingly tell how your proposal will help a customer, in a way the competition can't, you have a business problem. Not a communications problem.

When Not to Speak

The power of silence is underestimated, and this goes for both silence during a conversation and the skill to avoid certain topics. Raising your volume by lowering your decibels is exactly about this. A KA manager cannot simply bully their way around when they aren't heard. Confrontations will be frequent, both with the customer and within your company. In every case, it's necessary to question the need for the confrontation. The benefits of raising a potentially divisive topic need to outweigh the drawbacks. A very good tool to quickly review any upcoming conversation is the THINK method:

> T: Is it true?
>
> H: Is it helpful? Is it in line with your counterpart's interests?
>
> I: Is it inspiring? Will you get buy-in from the other party? Or will they turn defensive?
>
> N: Is it necessary? What will be accomplished? What exactly will the receiver need to do with the information you are sharing?
>
> K: Is it kind? Is it communicated in a respectful, clear way?

Alan Redpath, a British evangelist, first introduced THINK several decades ago, and it is still highly relevant for any business communication.

There are times when our own feelings demand we speak up: frustration, self-esteem, and so on are perfectly good reasons for engaging, but it has to be done while adhering to sound business awareness. And if the expected outcome isn't going to make a big impact in your life, it might be good to think twice.

If there isn't something in it for the counterpart, the conversation is likely to go nowhere.

A KA manager had just taken a new role in a major global information-technology company at one of the smaller overseas branches. The role carried responsibility for a few local key accounts which were significant in size but dwarfed by the global scale of the company. The KA manager had recently been appointed to the role, albeit having several years of KAM experience prior to this role. One of the customers was complaining about a product that her predecessor had sold them that they thought was unsuitable for their needs. The KA manager quickly realized that this was the case and a much more advanced version of the software was required to accomplish what the customer was looking for. It was a yearly contract and the company didn't allow for breaking the contract mid-term. For a new KA manager, it would be difficult to build credibility internally if this contract was terminated.

A meeting was planned to propose an upgrade, costing hundreds of thousands more. As expected, the customer was furious on hearing that to solve the problem, a more expensive contract had to be signed.

Knowing this, having experienced similar situations in the past, the KA manager stated the facts and clearly outlined the proposal. Then, when the customer got upset, blaming her predecessor for the error, and the company, and lamenting the situation, she remained quiet. She nodded in agreement and occasionally, expressed regret about the situation, but she did not interrupt the customer nor, at this point, insist on a solution. The silence helped in slowly defusing the situation, allowing the emotions out before the discussion could be moved on to solution mode. The solution was eventually an upgrade, at a very favorable price, resulting in a satisfied customer.

Written Communication

After being overrun by the fast food culture, slow food had a revival led by people who were fed up with the global blandness of fast food and processed food in general. I hope there is a similar revival of slow writing and reading. Less and less time and focus are put into writing and reading long form, be they books, memorandums, papers, and so on. A great deal of communication has moved to PowerPoint, e-mail, and text messages.

Read Between the Lines

Go deep into the message. Question the points it makes and form a hypothesis. For example, why did the sender decide to write this now, to me? Why this medium, why this tone? Why are these specific people being copied on the e-mail? Is there a message between the lines? Should I be wary of something?

This kind of conscious reading should be done without overanalyzing and without jumping to conclusions too quickly.

For example, an e-mail from someone you know that stands out as different from usual can mean many things: Someone else might have written the message; the sender might be in an abnormal state of mind; and so on. I once received an e-mail from a procurement partner whom I knew very well from years of doing business together. He wrote a very formal e-mail, a clue that the real message was not intended for me but for the management of his own company. He had to make them aware of what he was doing, and he did so by addressing that formal message to me. I made a great effort to respond appropriately, with his management team in mind as the main audience. I first discussed the situation with him over the phone to understand the big picture, how my response would be received, and how my message would solve his problem by encouraging his management team to have confidence in his actions.

Beware of Sensitive Information

With so much written communication exchanged, it is easy to become numb to confidential information that might be transmitted. What is day-to-day business for you can be a highly valuable strategic insight for a competitor. E-mails and online posts should be treated as public documents, and thinking twice before dispatching them is sound advice. E-mails and other messages are permanent and transferable; they can be read in days or months or years to come.

A good piece of advice is to visualize the e-mail on the front page of the *Financial Times*. If you are not comfortable with having it scrutinized in public, revise the text until it's something that will not embarrass you.

Preferably, send nonmodifiable documents. Several times, I have received spreadsheets that contain hidden cells and tabs with sensitive information. The sheets were likely made by an analyst, who created a complex sheet with hidden layers of information required for calculations, not considering that the sheet might be shared outside the company. Send a PDF version or an image file.

Orchestrating How and What You Communicate

Make sure your way of communicating follows a pattern and is consistent over time, and you have frequent touchpoints with the customer to ensure your message doesn't fade due to long periods of silence.

Frequent touchpoints, calls, e-mails, and messages—not only when a major issue arises—will make your action and thought path easier to follow. Especially, follow up after the event, conveying positive news of resolution and mitigation where relevant. Build trust with a combination of person-to-person communication with your counterpart at the customer company and communication with a wider audience, using a variety of tools.

Particularly when it comes to digital communications, the KA manager has to make extra effort to check the pulse, sensing where the customer is. The mental state of the counterpart will reveal a lot. Videoconferences mask a lot of this, as the dynamics between the agent isn't easy to pick up during a conference call. Video calls work for small groups; three to four participants allow for active participation and constructive discussions. After this, when the group increases, the level of disengagement increases, and participants will drift away by any minor distraction.

Sales Persona

And let's talk about your sales persona: how the various stakeholders in the buying organization perceive you. This persona is built from several identities that project onto you, the representative of your company. The company you work for will influence how others see you, as well as the products or services you provide through the procurement space. In addition, your position as sales manager will add to their perception of your persona, and finally, you, as an individual, will complete the picture.

Samir Majumdar[1] created a list of five sales profiles, stereotypes, that are handy for creating awareness of how the different stakeholders in the customer organization might see you. From the honest technical expert, "top tier Tom," to the eager closer of deals, "Cole the calculating closer," people will unknowingly classify salespeople into stereotypes and project traits on them.

Because your communication is going to affect your persona, strengthen or change it, and keeping close attention on the overall picture makes sense.

The tech team might see you as a friendly and helpful expert who contributes to their work with integrity. The legal team views you as someone eager to close deals with little else to offer, and the back office sees you as a goofy order taker who mainly wines and dines the procurement team. Be aware of this, and make sure that you prevent these projections from becoming too strong. It is easy to become too deeply personified, and it becomes a vicious circle that is difficult to get out of. If your sales persona is too strong, it will be difficult to achieve a promotion to a more senior role.

Make sure you get private time with stakeholders, especially if you meet them in group settings, because you need a decent amount of direct

---

[1] S. Majumdar. August 17, 2020. "Top 5 Distinct Sales Personas and How They Fit in Your Business," Veloxy.

contact with as many stakeholders as possible. It makes a difference. Catch up during breaks, ask them questions, and find ways to connect. They will then be less likely to form a stereotypical image of you.

Document Everything

Yes, it might be a requirement of the company. Yes, it might be annoying. But it is a good investment for you to meticulously document important information, so better to make it a relatively painless habit.

Most decisions and actions make sense at the time we make them, but this clarity will fade soon. Time kills the logic that was used for making the decision. Have you ever thought "What was I thinking?" and feel distant from your younger self? That happens to everybody.

Decisions are made with many influencing factors, most of which will be forgotten with time. The job requires constant decision making, often in a rush and with limited information at hand. Information is not just a single item, but the true value comes from the context that it is in and the circumstances why and how it was created. Information is enhanced by combining it with other information and ultimately using it to make decisions.[2]

The fast pace of business and the huge amount of information cause issues with correctly documenting information; there is just too much of it. And when documenting it correctly, if it is out of context, it will lose value. Equally, overload of information makes it impossible to retrieve it due to the total amount stored. The constantly lower cost of storage means that we store more.

Most likely, there are CRM systems that capture the main information, documents, and possibly communication trails. But much more subtle and detailed information is needed to be successful as a KA manager.

Create a Paper Trail and Sharpen Your Memory

To manage this constant flurry of decisions, it makes sense to create paper trails. The stressful environment we operate in renders it impossible to

---

[2] K.A. Megill. 2005. *Corporate Memory* (Munich: K.G. Saur Velag GmbH).

remember all decisions and logic over time. For everybody's benefit, it is useful to be able to easily access the history of the issue. Recalling what happened during previous negotiation rounds before embarking on new ones is a good practice, as well as reviewing past quality issues when a new one emerges. These are very subtle information, interpretations, and context to what happened. In addition to being aware of the technical circumstances (maybe the issue is a long-standing one), the correspondence and type of resolution are important to keep in mind. On countless occasions, I have reviewed my files on past decisions and been puzzled by them. Having the documents, e-mails, and all else that was stored did not enlighten me as to how we ended up with the agreement that we did. Often pricing decisions, if done by the KA manager, falls into this category. A single price does not merit the documentation and approvals a multiyear contract does, so it will easily be done without all logic documented. Often the strategic considerations that are influencing a decision will later be forgotten, such as the need to pre-empt a competitor or the logic of first gaining business share and then investing in suitable production capabilities.

During a multiyear contract with a key account, a new product was launched. It was business gained in a new geographical area, which fit very well with the strategic intent of the company to expand geographically by constructing a greenfield plant or by acquiring a smaller local company. Having a foothold with a major customer before this strategic move was considered critical. This new deal would provide good insight into the operational customs in the country and form connections with the local team of the customer. So a competitive price was given, despite the margins being unacceptably low.

However, two years later, the market conditions worsened and the company abandoned the plan to enter the new market. And this one product was still under contract for years, so supply could not be just stopped. And the background for this decision faded gradually within the organization, and eventually when the contract came to be renegotiated, the only one remaining with the recollection of this logic was the KA manager.

Needless to say, everything needs to be digital and accessible on the road.

CRM systems can be extremely frustrating and a thorn in the side of the sales team. But, at the same time, they provide real value. For your benefit, keep a good system for managing the customer relationship, combined with the CRM and systems that you created for yourself to fill the gaps.

The value of the system lies not in the data but in the history of your relationships with stakeholders. So design it with this in mind: as a support for you rather than an administrative burden.

Finally, if you have a very good memory, it will be of tremendous assistance in any sales role. Remembering details that are not captured in any system—names of people, conversations, past events, and product details—all of these give a strong impression and help connect with the customer. Improving your memory is a hard thing to do but not impossible. Stress and rushing are factors that weaken memory.[3] In addition to the direct effects of stress on cognitive functions, there is a tendency to rush when there is too much going on. A KA manager needs to make decisions and communicate them independently of what happens around them. Running around an airport while deciding on compensation for a quality claim will not register well in your memory.

Know Your Customer, Part 2

We have all been surprised by people's reactions when we bring bad news. Sometimes, they react as if it isn't a big deal, and other times, they react as if it is the end of the world. Countless times, we have heard, "It came out of the blue," when a relationship ends or people lose their job.

Many of these events could have been foreseen, but we weren't aware of them. Maybe, we missed some minor signal or didn't connect with someone who had insight into what was about to happen.

---

[3] F. Bermudez-Rattoni. 2007. *Neural Plasticity and Memory* (Boca Raton: CRC Press).

A manufacturing company supplies components for a customer who performs the final assembly before shipping the final product to end users. Do you, as the KA manager, know whether the components you supply are for just-in-time assembly or will be stocked? Is the component critical for completing the final product or can small changes be made that bypass shortage of this specific configuration of the product. Are you the sole supplier? Has your procurement counterpart got something personal at stake that would affect their reaction to bad news? Is this a specific delivery for a key project that has the attention of top management, making any delay reflect badly on your company and your procurement counterpart? Will the delay offer an opportunity for the customer to test a competitor or give the customer more power in an ongoing negotiation?

When structuring the communications plan, all these considerations need to be taken into account, and if you can get more insight, do it. Here, the strong network within the customer company is where to look for the precious insights that will help you succeed.

In addition to the advice given earlier, there are other aspects of the KA manager's job that are crucial to the success of the job. Advice on these aspects can be found in the following two chapters on how to maintain your excitement about the job and how to keep your customer happy to continue working with you for many years.

Summary

Effective communication plays a major role for rock star KA managers. There are multiple forms of communication; such as verbal and written communication, orchestrating the message, administration of information, and awareness of how the counterpart sees the messenger. In business, clear and simple language is preferred. Storytelling enhances the message, so it is a powerful tool to learn.

Knowing when to remain silent is an often overlooked skill; the THINK method helps evaluate if something needs to be said. Letting our emotions take over results in messages that ought not to have been sent. Written correspondence holds significant weight as it is permanent, so it is essential to be mindful of the potential pitfalls that can arise if not handled carefully. Orchestrate the communication, including frequent touchpoints, to keep your counterpart up-to-date when there are no issues. How we communicate directly impacts how stakeholders perceive us, easily categorizing the KA manager into a specific sales persona. Understanding how the stakeholders in the customer organization see us will aid in our interaction and relationship with them.

Keeping meticulous records and documenting past correspondence prove invaluable in navigating and preventing potential problems in customer interactions. Having a well-organized paper trail, or CRM trail, helps manage all the moving parts involved in the complex process of key account management. A great memory will be a tremendous help for anyone in a commercial role; recalling information helps connect people and build a professional and respected figure toward the customer.

CHAPTER 9

Love and Pride

Overview

- The fuel that drives the KA manager is love and pride for the profession.
- Integrity is the building block to gain respect and credibility.
- Bringing bad news and engaging with the customer during tough times require courage and a long view.

Fuzzy

This is likely the fuzziest chapter of the book. Love and pride are the fuel that makes the job so rewarding and provides you with the energy to get up in the morning with a smile on your face. This is what, essentially, makes some account managers star performers and others not. It makes the job exciting, the days enjoyable, and the customers happy.

To be able to cope with the early morning customer calls or late Friday afternoon requests requires something more than a paycheck at the end of the month. Without passion for the client, the tasks will become heavy, and over time, this burden will start to show. Your lack of enthusiasm for the job and the clients will start to be evident. Your complaints get more frequent, and your energy drops lower and lower. This is a vicious circle and not what successful account management is about. The real, deep magic of account management is to bring the human touch to the otherwise sterile relationship between two companies.

As in any relationship, each customer will have flaws, idiosyncrasies, and ways of working that you won't like. Along with the good times, there will be painful experiences, and accepting and managing these are turning points in the relationship. Empathy is an absolute must for managing these difficulties, as is having genuine, positive feelings for the customer. Don't work for someone or something you don't respect, whether an industry that doesn't share your values or a customer with questionable practices. If you don't like consumerism, don't work for the fashion industry. If your counterpart at one of your accounts is, in your opinion, unbearable, then do all that it takes to change accounts. If you consider the procurement processes of the industry inhuman, then change the industry. Staying in a situation that isn't in sync with your values will be draining and do nothing to help your career or personal development; it will just torpedo your ambitions. Even if it pays well. Revert to something where your passion can come into play and you can love your client and rock the world.

A good friend told me that when you start working with a new account, give the new customer one month to fall in love with you. If you manage this, then the actual job can start.

Consider your situation when starting the job, and see where you fit in. Having love for, and taking pride in, the KA manager position should spring from a solid foundation of technical and soft skills that, in turn, build the kind of self-confidence, love, and pride needed for the job.

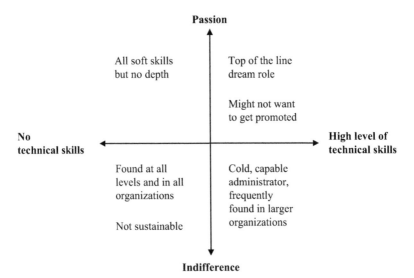

Figure 9.1 As you settle into the role, be mindful to not slide into the bottom-left quadrant

Hard and Soft Skills

You will need to bring something to the table in terms of skills. Be the go-to person discussed in Chapter 1, "Know Them as You Know Yourself," that has something to offer beyond talk. Skills can be anything that is appreciated and valued, making you stand out from the rest, such as a deep understanding of the customer's technology and business, negotiation skills, and people skills, or a combination of these.

Passion is how you feel deep inside about what you are doing. It radiates to create a good work environment that empowers you and your stakeholders.

Save some love also for the end users of whatever value chain you are in. Even if the product you work with is a rivet in a metal plate for an aluminum boat, try to relate and bond with the people purchasing these boats and see what makes them tick.

Integrity

The following is a definition of integrity, commonly attributed to C. S. Lewis:

Integrity is doing the right thing, even when no one is watching.[1]

KAM is the obligation to engage and interact again and again with the same customer, especially when the customer is deeply dissatisfied. This is surprisingly common in industries where high capital intensity and few large players limit new entrants, and thus the customers cannot easily change suppliers. This also occurs in more fluid industries where there is inertia about making the changes necessary to work with a big account. As an example, where a bank finds switching IT suppliers to be risky and resource-heavy, the bank's procurement contact will be tied to the supplier's KA manager for the long term.

---

[1] According to the C.S. Lewis Foundation, this quote is misattributed to Lewis. It is, rather, a paraphrase of words taken from Charles Marshall's book *Shattering the Glass Slipper*, www.cslewis.org/aboutus/faq/quotes-misattributed/.

This easily leads to toxic relationships and long-term conflicts. With your values in place, and trust built up over time, your engagement will be more than just doing a job. And it will show.

This might sound obvious, as integrity is beneficial to every job. But I believe that for this specific role, integrity has an added value that increases the goodwill of the company as a whole, and does so more than many other jobs can. KA managers will find themselves in controversial situations that they might not even condone. To be able to do this requires that the customer trusts that the KA manager has done everything that could be done in difficult situations. Portraying consistently high integrity and showing a deep engagement are fundamental in overcoming those difficult moments.

Don't lie and don't collect skeletons in the closet. This will complicate the relationship and make engagement constrained. Lies are easy ways out of a difficult conversation, but will compromise integrity.

With a one-off sale, the consequences of what is said might not be impactful for the future, but in an ongoing relationship, all the white lies act like booby traps for future navigation because the customer will remember them.

Providing reasons for pricing is one of the tricky communication exercises. The philosophy of market pricing versus cost-based pricing is understandable. Many businesses want to apply market pricing to their sales but cost-based pricing on their purchases. All KA managers have been challenged on this by procurement teams who break down the costs in order to unsettle the pricing decisions of the seller.

An easy way out is to offer a vague answer about some high cost base or other, or a plant that has a low output. Don't fall into this trap; you will get caught sooner or later. Instead develop a solid, relatively honest answer that is in line with your integrity and aligned with your company. This does not mean to be blunt, but to formulate an answer that stands being challenged and is in line with what your values are. And stand by it.

Taking a Beating and Still Standing

Conveying bad news, in a good way, is a form of art. Some tools can be learned, as we saw in Chapter 7, "The Sweet Deal." Even with all things done right, the counterpart will still be affected, and your relationship tested. But with the correct message, and trust in the messenger, the counterpart is able to take the message and do what is needed within their organization to manage the situation. Make their job easier by communicating the right information. Don't be tempted to make your life temporarily painless by withholding information or not telling the truth.

Engaging in a lot of such conversations will affect you. One of the harder parts of the job is taking a beating for your employer. Burnouts, stress, and dissatisfaction with the job are caused by stressful situations and tough conversations where you might not agree with the message or you need to protect someone else in your company. Manage integrity by telling the truth without necessarily saying everything.

Never take the road of blaming or resenting the customer. The role dynamics between the seller and buyer are what they are. Accept this situation without lamenting the power imbalance and giving in to the temptation to compromise integrity.

A strong, positive relationship between you and your counterpart will make your work much easier and can be achieved through long-term trust and a build-up of goodwill with the customer.

The Lone Voice of the Customer

KA managers are tasked with the lonely job of delivering bad news, but the procurement role can be as lonely as the KA manager's. This is often because the main channel of communication for the customer is through the procurement team.

Passionate account managers stand up for their customers, defend these close allies, and speak for them in any forum. Taking a stand for them and defending their cause is just part of the job. The decision makers of your company, who control resources, strategy, and the priorities to focus on, need to hear the position of all the parties, and you are the customer's voice.

If the account managers aren't standing up for their customers, there is little support for the customers elsewhere, and management will start to view those customers as less important, voiceless entities that might be forgotten among louder voices speaking for other customers.

Speak up; the same rules apply as for communication with the customer. Strong integrity combined with good communication skills makes you an articulate, trustworthy, and, in the long term, effective asset for your company.

Summary

Passion, love, and pride are ingredients for a KA manager to not only succeed but also enjoy and have happy customers. Without genuine enthusiasm, the tasks become burdensome and impossible to sustain performance and customer satisfaction for a longer time.

The relationship between the KA manager and the customer is like any other relationship; it has ups and downs. Dealing with difficult situations requires empathy and genuine care for the customer. It's essential to work for someone or something that aligns with your values to avoid draining all your energy.

Integrity plays a crucial role in successful account management. Building trust and maintaining a good reputation are vital, especially in challenging situations where difficult decisions must be made. Honesty and authentic engagement with the customer are necessary for a strong, long-term relationship. This comes into play when delivering bad news. It is an art that requires skillful communication and trust between the parties involved. While it might be tough, the KA manager must convey the message honestly and help the customer manage the situation. Being the lone voice of the customer is part of the KA manager's responsibility. Advocating for the customer, standing up for their needs, and representing their interests within the company are crucial for maintaining a positive relationship and supporting the customer's requirements.

CHAPTER 10

Keeping It Fresh

Overview

- Over time, KA managers product, value added benefits, operational often get comfortable with stable customer relationships, which easily lead to fading relationships and loss of business.
- Innovation mitigates this decline—in product, operational efficiency, and any other field where improvements can be found.
- The rupture doesn't come suddenly, even if there are account managers who are surprised when the customer says goodbye. There are usually signs of this beforehand; spotting them gives time to correct the course.

Our Lazy Minds

Over time, we get lazy; our bodies and brains are designed to conserve energy, not spend it without purpose. Our mind strives for balance. We become more efficient at the activities we regularly do, and with experience, we use less energy over time for the same work. The flip side is that we might cut corners and slack off.

The key is to harness this laziness and turn it into creativity, to push the comfort zone when things become settled. The question is how to use the time saved by this increased productivity and motivate yourself to remain relevant. Innovating and creating new challenges are a mental workout. Successful people do this to keep motivated and improve performance. In account management, a new customer–supplier relationship starts with high motivation, big expectations, and a bunch of energy. When both parties are comfortable with each other, the daily operations become standard, and the relationship starts to cool off.

Helena Åkerlund studied this phenomenon and aptly named it "fading customer relationships."[1] She describes several unfortunate outcomes of key account relationships, going from massive crashes to slow deaths. The crashes are best avoided by the advice given in the other parts of this book, such as crisis management and ethical ways of doing business. Slow fading is different and often unnoticed.

When you work with the same account for a long period, you will inevitably face stagnation. The tangible benefits of strong and long-lasting relationships trump the risk of stagnation in most companies. Making changes for the sake of change is not effective. You need to fight the stagnation that limits your progress, experience, and, consequently, your career progression. This applies to both sides of the relationship. Stagnation will prevent your procurement counterpart from getting the most out of the supplier, which will lead to a growing dissatisfaction with the supplier and the eventual rupture of business.

Let's focus on what you can do to avoid involuntarily losing a customer, which is a disaster for the business and you, professionally. Increasingly, the business-to-business market is moving beyond focusing on the core products and services to actually solving problems for, and helping, the customer.[2] Seems obvious and like sound advice? In reality, it's not so straight forward. Since the selling company's products and services are fixed, offering something beyond what you are currently offering is not done without great effort and will require change. Still, it's a battle worth fighting, because when a supplier relies only on delivery of the same product, two things happen. First, discussions will likely revolve around price. Second, the supplier is more prone to be dislodged by the competition as there are few attributes to compete on. This is commoditization, so stay clear of it.

---

[1] H. Åkerlund. 2004. *Fading Customer Relationships* (Helsinki: Swedish School of Economics and Business Administration).

[2] H. Grove, K. Sellers, R. Ettenson, and J. Knowles. August 1, 2018. "Selling Solutions Isn't Enough," MIT Sloan Management Review.

Not Just Plain Vanilla Innovation

Bringing something new to the business relationship on a continual basis requires a few basics to be in place. The first two rules are listening to the customer and sharing the success with them. Listening beyond what is said and really understand what the customer needs helps you succeed in their space. It is important to focus on their world as too often innovation departments become self-centered and focus on tinkering with the product. This produces a constant flow of incremental and indifferent new features that have little value for the customers. It is inevitable because this is the easiest way to "innovate." However, it will not be met by enthusiasm by customers. The second is allowing your counterpart to shine and take part in what is accomplished. Make the process a team work and get them onto the innovation team. Let them take part in the credit within their company; internal communication teams love good stories of innovation workshops and partnership. This is a guaranteed booster for your relationship—and a ticket to participate in new innovation events.

A word of caution when innovating—while creativity is a must, there are boundaries. Socially, within the customer's tribe, there are limits that it is wise to stay clear of. All groups have taboos and sensitive areas, and when innovating, it is easy to tumble across the border of what is good innovation and what is not. Anything that affects the brand or changes that would impact the identity and values of the customer are best to stay clear of.

A new receptionist who felt that change was needed in a rather dull office decided to turn all lampshades upside down. She did this for no particular reason, and the effect was a bit different light profile when most of the illumination was now directed upwards. This somehow impacted the office staff strongly, and it became *the* topic around the coffee machine. The change was not appreciated; it somehow touched a sore nerve in the office culture.

Without realizing it, the new receptionist did changes that overstepped the social norms of the office and a minor, and reversible, change became a problem within the team.

Core Product or Service

The most obvious point to focus the innovation on is the actual product or service that is delivered, but it is one of the hardest things to do. The fact is that it is probably already finely tuned and your company has a lot of people working on it, from product management to R&D and marketing—likely not a low-hanging fruit to focus on.

The primary way you could contribute to finding new product innovations is through your access to information coming directly from the customer, which gives you a perspective that others don't necessarily have.

An easier way is to find untapped opportunities for cross-selling products that your company currently offers. Or propose minor tweaks to existing products to fit them to your customer's specific needs. This approach to innovation requires keeping up-to-date on the status of the industry and actively scoping for opportunities.

Value Added Benefits

Products and services are often well defined and information is publicly available, while the value added benefits tied to the offering are not that transparent. Value added benefits are everything offered beyond the core product and service, for example; financing solutions, co-marketing at events, joint strategic projects, and how you, as an account manager, respond to your customer's calls. Clearly, the distinction is not black and white; some value added benefits are in some kind tied to the product, and some become so over time as they evolve into *hygiene factors*. These are features that were originally available only as a premium, but over time, evolve into must-haves to such and extent that their absence causes dissatisfaction. Electric windows in cars or free Internet in hotels, for example, used to be premium options but have become features that, will severly diminish the value of the offering if missing.

Keeping up-to-date on what these services are and how they change is not tied to the business or product and can be copied from other businesses. KA managers in similar industries can have good practices worth adopting. New technology for simplifying work or just great customer service practices can be found in any industry.

Operational Improvements

Innovation also includes improvements in systems and operational procedures. Innovation on contract terms and pricing models can have an impact well beyond what was expected. For example, a transparent pricing model can transform the relationship with a customer, making it more intimate and dynamic. A creative joint-marketing campaign will similarly tie the companies together, potentially create stronger brand value, and lead the KA manager to form bonds with new people in the customer organization.

For the operations of any company, cost-saving innovations are always in high demand. Sometimes, especially in manufacturing, this is stipulated in the contract, requiring activities that will result in a yearly percentage reduction in the purchase price. Nobody says no to cost savings. However, this should not be the only focus area, it's really just business as usual.

External Change

There are constant, gradual improvements and changes to the way of doing business that make companies more agile and effective. They come from outside and can cause huge disruption to the way of doing business.

The potential for innovating in this space is massive. You are in a unique position to look at the customer's world from the outside, with a deep insight into their operations and culture. Here, it is perfectly acceptable to copy something from what you read or see in your everyday life. When you meet someone new from a different industry, a perfect networking topic to discuss is "What is a great innovation that you have seen that is not directly product related?"

Innovation is often a very strong driver for a supplier in the business-to-business space to retain business year in and year out. The risk customers take if they leave an innovative supplier is that they will miss potential new innovations. Explore your ideas and do it with passion and curiosity to go beyond what your company currently offers.

Bring a Buddy

The use of creativity should be expanded to other aspects of the supplier–customer relationship. For example, change the location for meetings; introduce colleagues who are experts in their field; and add inspiring work practices to the interaction. You have a vast pool of great talent in your company, who are often very eager to meet customers and have a ton of insight to share.

Connecting experts, business leaders, or even outside experts to showcase something specific will raise the quality of the meeting. There is a model for this way of working, depicting two opposite relationships.[3] The bow-tie relationship refers to a relationship in which the only contact between the companies is limited to the salesperson and the procurement person. The diamond relationship refers to a relationship that is expanded to include multiple touchpoints, and a network is formed between the entities.

This shift allows for a more nuanced relationship and better mutual understanding. Plus, it takes away all the coordination and project management from the KA manager and, importantly, distributes the responsibilities, which otherwise lie solely on the KA manager. Still, there is a risk you will stand alone when things go wrong if not careful, so it is not a bulletproof get-out-of-jail card.

Keep in mind the risks with this kind of relationship. Unfortunately, not all people have people skills and may lack not only the skills but also the interest in representing a company professionally. Orchestrating and managing these encounters can be like herding cats but still worth the try. Are you surprised to see how defensive people get when you give them advice on client interaction?

The way to achieve self-sustaining collaboration is for the KA manager to orchestrate mixed networks between the company's and the customer's teams. This lifts the collaboration above the individual, and the organizations form deeper connections. An example of this is a product development project where experts with very specific and deep knowledge

---

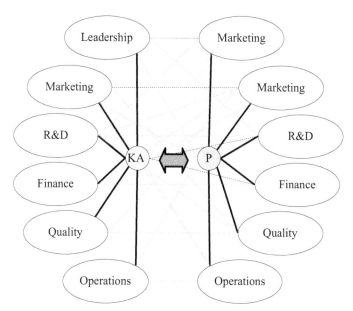

Figure 10.1 Orchestrating with your team to connect with the customer on multiple levels. KA = KA manager, P = purchasing

share their expertise with the customer. These kinds of projects work well for technically advanced products. Co-marketing, operations, and logistics are equally well adapted. Six Sigma, Scrum, and other project management concepts are sought-after skills, and if you can dedicate these experts to a customer project, there is certainly value to it.

Most of the time, initiatives come from the customer and make it much easier to get buy-in from your management team than the other way around. To gain the buy-in from the customer requires a very strong relationship and an attractive value proposition.

A key customer who had a very strong position in western Europe but was weak globally had a problem. Globally, the supplier was much larger than the customer, and in North America, the supplier was the market leader. The customer's problem was that their supply chain was struggling in North America; they were small and didn't have the expertise or resources to drive change. On the other hand, the supplier had much better insight into the logistics field in the

(Continues)

(Continued)

> country and skillful experts on the team. The KA manager, knowing the situation, was able to initiate a project with the scope of co-purchasing logistics, including warehousing, where demand seasonality made it possible to utilize some of the services both companies needed jointly. The benefits were clear, but a big hurdle was convincing the customer's logistics team of the benefits. Together with the global buyer, who was the KA manager's main counterpart, they managed to convince the team.

Keeping a private idea funnel for yourself will be useful. Any idea, small or big, feasible or improbable, is welcome. At the best, this will result in projects, and if not, it will be a great conversation topic that could unlock areas of interest for both parties and give insight into the customer's challenges and difficulties.

To manage this efficiently, share the ideas you have with the customer and keep track of the reaction you get. You will see which areas are of interest and which not. Vice versa, keep track of customer suggestions and also those that don't get traction immediately. This way of capturing ideas can be formal, using a CRM, or using any other tool that can keep track of the funnel.

Spotting Danger

> *Scenario*: A large customer of a Fortune 500 company, known for tough negotiations and cost pressure, was on the other side of the table. The customer was important—in fact one of the largest for the business unit and classified as a key account. The yearly contract negotiation was ongoing, as it was mid-November. Despite attempts, the KA manager had not been able to secure a longer term contract with the customer.
>
> Pressure was on, as always, and the customer demanded considerable price concessions, without much in return, and with strict contract terms, as always.

It was business as usual after the first round of offers when the KA manager and the VP of Sales paid a visit to the customer to pursue the negotiation. Being reasonably well prepared, with the possibility of ceding on price and on some of the terms, they were convinced this would be enough to seal the deal.

All went well during the meeting and small talk at the coffee machine, but that changed quickly when they sat down at the negotiating table. The customer informed the shocked KA manager and accompanying VP that the business had been awarded elsewhere. There was no possibility of having further discussions, and only yes–no to a minor part of what remained. And the contract would be a tactical, spot business agreement with no commitments beyond what was ordered. This was a token gesture to allow the customer to keep the pulse of the market with continued supply and be a potential backup in case of failure with the new supplier.

What to learn here? After years of working with the customer, the sales team had turned a deaf ear to the subtle signals that could have saved the deal.

After all, the procurement team does calculations and analysis on a daily basis to de-risk and broaden supply. So the subtle signals should have been seen well in advance before a loss of business. Examples are:

- You have poor contact with your main counterpart. Hard to get in touch, don't stay in touch. They avoid meetings and are generally too busy to engage with you.
- You lack joint opportunities and projects, especially if these were happening previously.
- Incidents of quality or performance issues start to make the supporters within the customer's organization less enthusiastic about you.
- Your competition makes strategic moves within the industry. Reading about new product lanches, new investments, and hires can indicate that there will be bad news coming. There might not be any signs of a big shift happening; the customer will keep

this quiet when they have made the final decision to switch suppliers.

Spot these and know how to prepare. Make sure that the procurement team feels that they are winning, that they fear missing out on future innovations, and that the relationship is constantly kept fresh.

Summary

Over time, our minds tend to become lazy, seeking a comfortable balance and conserving energy. With increased efficiency and experience in our work, there's a temptation to slack off and cut corners when it comes to the customer. The key is to channel this laziness into creativity, pushing ourselves out of our comfort zone and finding ways to stay motivated and relevant. Innovation and creating new challenges act as a mental workout to keep us motivated and improve our performance.

Helena Åkerlund's study on "fading customer relationships" highlights the potential decline of key account relationships over time; this is something that a KA has direct control over.

To avoid involuntarily losing a customer, it's essential to focus on continuous innovation and adding value beyond the core product and service. Listening to the customer's needs and involving them in the success of innovations strengthen the relationship. Innovation can target almost any area, such as product enhancements, services, and operational improvements.

Expanding the customer connection to involve a broad team and orchestrating mixed networks between the company and the customer deepen collaboration and understanding. Monitoring subtle signs of deterioration in customer relationships is crucial, allowing for intervention and course correction before it's too late. To stay ahead, it is good to keep a private idea funnel and then share ideas with the customer.

CHAPTER 11

KAM

A Ladder to the Top

Overview

- The KA manager role is senior, caring for a company's most important customers.
- Job openings for KA managers look for a palette of soft skills on top of work experience, education, and industry insight. Often, familiarity with the customers is requested.
- The career progression of a KA manager is usually either continuing within the KAM department or moving within the commercial space; business development and commercial excellence are paths often taken.

A Good Career

The last step is to understand the career of a KA manager, from getting a job to moving on to other roles. The purposefulness of a role is often influenced by what the next career step is after that. The KA manager job can be a "job for life," moving jobs between similar roles that provide an excellent professional identity; with years or even decades of thoughtful experience, the accumulated network, skills gained, and overall mastery of the job make it satisfying. A mix of analytical thinking and customer engagement, corporate travel, and a combination of hunting for new customers and farming existing accounts make it a multifaceted role.

Interviewees for this book range from people who have moved on to CEO roles in less than five years and people who became expert KA managers by moving positions and gaining thought leadership and customer ownership from decades of work in the role.

There is a wide range of KAM positions. The requirements for candidates vary significantly between different companies. It is common to come across job titles that essentially serve as synonyms for the KA manager role, such as Prime Named Account Executive, Client Director, and Named Account Manager, and other variations that reflect the creativity of human resource (HR) consultants designing organizational structures. However, it is important to not be misled by the job title alone, as a genuine KA manager role possesses certain defining characteristics. Rather than focusing on the title, focus on the job content. Some roles are junior, with a strong component of hunting for new customers, and then there are senior roles with the responsibility of one or two customers who purchase for hundreds of millions or billions of U.S. dollars. And these senior roles carry a lot of weight within their organizations. For demanding positions, the title will be adjusted accordingly, such as senior key account (KA) manager, global KA manager, or account director. The role of vice president of key accounts denotes a leadership position within the department. As job requirements differ, so does the compensation. As of 2023, it is not uncommon for top KA managers to earn salaries above $200,000.

A genuine KAM role is senior and has got true responsibility for the most important customers of a company. This kind of responsible company would not let that into the hands of someone who has yet to demonstrate their abilities and prove their technical skills. A mistake will be costly as losing even one single top customer can wreak havoc on a business. Additionally, the candidate for this kind of demanding role will need a broad toolbox of skills and a large network to be able to serve these top customers efficiently.

What They Expect From a KA Manager

There are a few essential considerations to help you evaluate and navigate the positions and enable you to effectively assess the caliber of the role.

Experience

You will need relevant work experience for a KAM role. It is rarely an entry-level job. The usual request is a candidate who has been in at least one prior commercial job and gained a track record. This track record should show the portfolio of skills that the candidate has and evidence of dealing with multitude of situations that will occur on the job. Building networks takes years, especially within the industry. For example, trade shows can be powerful networking events but take place infrequently.

The shortest job experience required that I have seen for a job posting is two years. And this is an exception. Most jobs demand more than four years, and some companies require over eight years of relevant experience. The best starting place is to go through junior sales assignments; account executive positions are excellent entry roles. Customer support and other jobs with direct customer engagement are equally valued. Graduate programs where the first experiences are in business analyst roles are also excellent entry points from noncommercial jobs.

When it comes to requiring specific technical experience, the pharma industry takes the price for the most snobbish attitude to outsiders. Without a specific pharma-related education combined with experience in the field, anyone who desires to enter this field later in their career has really one realistic option, and that is to obtain a top MBA degree.

It is rare for recruiters not to require commercial experience from the candidate. And it is also rare that an internal candidate, except someone moving from junior business analyst or a graduate program, become a KA manager.

A common, maybe peculiar, request is the need for previous work experience with the account and having a network within the customer organization. And this often results in a job to be filled by a candidate from a competitor or peer who serves the same customer. A candidate with this experience is very quick to be efficient in the role. For the KA manager, a move like this will open doors to larger purchasing purses and possibly expand the area of responsibility geographically.

Hard Technical Skills

Many KA managers work for companies offering technically advanced products and services to well-informed customers. This makes know-how of the technology and product a must. The technical level does not need to be at par with the experts in the company but needs to be fluent in discussions of what is provided to the customer. And often, insight into what the customer sells and the business they are in is a requirement.

Another often-requested skill is proficiency with CRM systems. It can be an experience of any CRM, and in some cases, companies specify requirements for a specific type of CRM.

Other software skills are proficiency in spreadsheets, e-mail, and presentation programs. The role does not require exceptional skills, but as almost all businesses run on Microsoft Office, without this, a candidate will be lost in the day-to-day work.

Other hard skills that are frequently requested are:

- *Finance and pricing*: Having responsibility for the top customers of a company carries a direct impact on financials, and you need a good grasp of the finance part to succeed. Pricing is often the responsibility of a KA manager and is a powerful tool in the commercial portfolio, directly influencing both revenue and profitability. In addition, many contract terms influence the company's financial statements. Payment terms and stock levels impact working capital, and quality and service levels impact profitability.
- *Project management*: To successfully lead a portfolio of customer projects requires excellent project management skills. Formal project management qualifications and experience with major projects will be a plus when applying for a job.
- *Presentation skills*: Delivering compelling slide-based presentations to a small audience is the bread and butter of pitching an idea. The KA manager's day is peppered with internal and customer presentations to convey ideas and get support. Storytelling, logical thinking, and an eye for simple and attractive visuals are components that form great presentation skills.

Education

The most sought-after degrees are bachelor's degrees in technology and in business. Rarely is a masters's degree required, although they will provide bonus points for the candidate. In most industries, specific in-depth education isn't required, except for highly technical fields such as pharma. Education provides an entry ticket to the field and is secondary to experience and skills in the eye of recruiters.

Language Skills

In today's globalized business landscape, English has become the lingua franca of international commerce, and thus for numerous multinational corporations, proficiency in English is often sufficient for the job. However, the degree of local language proficiency and local market knowledge necessary for a KA manager role will vary depending on the industry and customer base.

In regions like the Netherlands and the Nordics, English proficiency is so prevalent that many corporations operate solely in English. Nevertheless, possessing knowledge of the local languages in these regions can still be advantageous. Conversely, in most other non-English-speaking areas, fluency in the local language becomes a prerequisite for success in the role. This is because effective communication and understanding of the local market dynamics and cultural nuances play a crucial role in building strong relationships with customers.

Therefore, while English proficiency is valuable in global business settings, it is essential to recognize the importance of local language skills.

Soft Skills for Real Rock Stars

The list of soft skills is long and carries a lot of weight in the selection process. Given that this entire book revolves around soft skills, there is no need to reiterate what has already been written. However, worth mentioning is a quantitative study conducted by the author, which examined the prevalence of key words in job postings for KA manager positions. By analyzing the most frequently used terms in the job requirements, the study shed light on the specific qualities and attributes that recruiting managers and recruiters seek in prospective candidates. This study provides valuable insights into the expectations and preferences of those responsible for hiring KA managers.

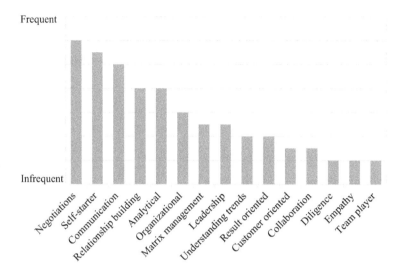

Figure 11.1 The prevalence of soft skills key words in open key account manager job posts (The EU, the United Kingdom, the United States, and Switzerland)

Where Are You Going?

As a career path, KAM is appreciated and teaches valuable skills. All commercial roles teach amazing skills that are fundamental for leadership roles in business. And all leadership roles are people roles in the end. The ability to influence, use soft power, lead projects, build teams, and lead people are skills learned in the KA manager job.

The business acumen of a KA manager, which was already required to get the job, will have improved, and financial dynamics will be well understood: pricing, contract terms, service level agreements, financial statements, and the order to cash process, to name a few. These are what make a business tick, and few people get a better view of this than the KA manager.

With strong, transferable skills, there are a few paths to choose from. A linear approach is to keep within the trade, moving on to higher stakes and responsibilities by changing companies or taking more demanding roles within the same company. This means gaining experience from different customers with bigger budgets, more complex geographies, and customers who are even more key to the business. As the accounts grow more complex and larger, the seniority increases, and the title will gain prefixes such as global and senior, and the title becomes director instead of manager. This path of higher responsibilities managing the accounts gives higher prestige, and the role can become very senior.

If moving to people management is a career goal, the progression to leading a team of KA managers is natural; however, it is often beneficial to have experience in several KA manager roles or one or two stints in other roles before taking this kind of job. Transitioning to other commercial roles is a natural progression; commercial excellence or business development requires skills similar to that of a KA manager. Transitioning into noncommercial roles will be a bigger threshold, especially if most of your career has been in KAM. Most move within the commercial field.

Decipher the Code

Facing a job posting for any role is daunting. Few applicants possess the skills of a unicorn that the postings often look for. Here, I have a few "typical" KAM requirements, from actual postings, with tips on what to look for and how to interpret it. However, responding to open positions has a low chance of success versus other ways of job hunting. If you already work as a KA manager with a few years of experience, your network will be the best path to a new job. Take an active interest in learning about other companies in the field while you are monitoring the competitive landscape. Using this insight, you can select companies that align with your interests. This could involve choosing a reputable company that supplies different products to your customers or exploring a new player entering the field. Another option is transitioning to a startup that values your customer contacts and experience—all depending on your risk tolerance.

If you are looking for your first KA manager job, have a sober look at the requirements, and try to see how your CV looks through the lens of a recruiter. If, in all honesty, you are far off, then try to get a stepping stone job, such as an entry-level sales or account manager position. Since every situation is unique, consider hiring a coach. Coaching is likely to yield significant benefits, making it a worthwhile investment.

When preparing for a job interview as a KA manager, it's essential to consider both role-specific inquiries and insightful general questions. Specifically, it's important to inquire about the job's history and the fate of its previous occupant. KAM departments frequently undergo restructuring, so if you're stepping into a newly formed team within a new organization, it has a lot more challenges than joining a well-functioning team. The history of the predecessor who held the role before could give insight into the promotional practices within the company if this was an internal promotion. Try to find out what happened that led to the departure. Speaking with them might provide you with the inside scoop.

The accounts that the role will be serving play a big part in job success and your own job satisfaction. Often, the accounts are named in the job posting; if not, they should be revealed latest during the first interview. As some KA manager roles serve less than three customers, the characteristics of the customers will influence the work almost as much as the company you work for. Once you have identified the customer or account you'll be working with, it is crucial to conduct thorough research on them, especially if they are unfamiliar to you. Dedicate the same level of effort and attention to understanding the customer as you would for the job itself.

Keep an eye out for weird requirements. Examples from actual job postings reveal a lot about the job:

- *"Full process compliance to achieve service excellence outcomes"*— A rules-based company, so don't expect too much autonomy.
- *"Manage the leads provided by the SDRs, carrying out from the presentation of the product to the closing of the offer"*— Contrary to the KA manager title, this particular role does not primarily focus on key accounts. If the number of accounts to be managed exceeds 10, then it is not a role that handles genuine key accounts.
- *Too much emphasis on MS Office capacities*—This probably means that the role is junior or a company that thinks computers are a new thing, and thus using a spreadsheet is something for a candidate to highlight. Both cases should merit probing into this during the interview.

- *A job posting filled with jargon and abbreviations*—Either this is a self-centric company which doesn't realize that its language is off-putting for an outside candidate or, alternatively, it could be a deliberate signal that the company prefers a candidate who is already familiar with the industry's insider terminology. There are instances where an internal candidate has already been chosen, but regulations or legal requirements necessitate public posting of the job. In such cases, it is unlikely that you will secure the position.
- *No travel required*—An indication that the job is junior or other reasons why seeing customers isn't required. Most KAM roles require 20 to 40 percent travel; less than this will remove a lot of the intimacy with the customers and local teams.

When examining a KA manager job posting, there are three crucial elements you should look for that define the role:

1. A clear description of how many customers, the role, and the responsibilities. A KA manager role should be easy to define clearly and the customers should not be a secret.
2. Requesting core KAM skills, such as negotiation, communication, and analytics, and solid understanding of finance and market analysis. They are looking for a candidate who is target driven and has excellent relationship-building skills and people skills.
3. Clarity on how much of the job is hunting for new business and how much is managing existing accounts. Some companies provide extra cash bonuses to KA managers for new customer acquisitions; signaling that this is something on top of the normal responsibilities.

The career path of a KA manager has to come out of passion, and then it is an extremely rewarding occupation. The balance of interacting with customers strategically, with dashes of finance, technology, negotiations, and operations, makes every day different. It is like a symphony of business, with just the right balance of crescendo, subtlety, adrenaline, and doing long-term good for someone else. Attractive, transferable skills are learned from the role, and if played well, they will aid tremendously in advancing a career in commercial roles.

An exceptionally successful KA manager, who has been able to shape a unique and strong position in the job market, summarized very well the essence of KAM:

> My job today is what it has been for a long time, building relationships and ensuring that what was sold was delivered on—not because it's in my job title or because I am measured on it, let alone paid for it, it's because that is the key to my survival as a sales professional and also the key to preserving and enhancing my reputation.

Summary

The career of a KA manager can be fulfilling and diverse, offering a multifaceted role that combines analytical thinking, customer engagement, and various exciting responsibilities. The requirements for a KA manager role differ between companies, and the job titles may vary, but the defining characteristics of a genuine KA manager position involve seniority and true responsibility for important customers.

To be successful as a KA manager, relevant work experience is crucial, usually requiring a track record in commercial roles or customer engagement positions. Technical skills related to the products or services offered by the company are essential, as well as proficiency in CRM systems and basic software applications. In terms of education, a bachelor's degree is often the minimum requirement.

Soft skills play a significant role in the selection process, and employers often seek candidates with qualities such as communication, negotiation, relationship-building, project management, and presentation skills. A study of job postings for KA manager positions revealed the most frequently sought-after soft skills.

In terms of career progression, successful KA managers usually advance by moving to more demanding jobs within KAM or moving to other commercial roles. The skills learned on the job are valuable and will be useful in a broad range of jobs.

It's essential to carefully evaluate job postings as they can contain red flags. What you want to see are three main points: clearly defined customer responsibilities, the need for core KAM skills, and a healthy dose of sales and business development.

Bibliography

Akerlof, G. 1970. "The Market for "Lemons": Quality Uncertainty and the Market Mechanism." *The Quarterly Journal of Economics* 84, no. 3, pp. 488–500.

Akerlof, G.A. and R.J. Shiller. 2009. *Animal Spirit: How Human Psychology Drives the Economy and Why It Matters for Global Capitalism.* Princeton University Press.

Åkerlund, H. 2004. *Fading Customer Relationships.* Helsinki: Swedish School of Economics and Business Administration.

Bermudez-Rattoni, F. 2007. *Neural Plasticity and Memory, From Genes to Brain Imaging.* Boca Raton: CRC Press.

Bhasin, H. March 20, 2019. "Four Types of Business Resources." *Marketing91.* www.marketing91.com/four-types-of-business-resources/.

Bollard, A., E. Larrea, A. Singla, and R. Sood. March 1, 2017. "The Next Generation Operating Model for the Digital World." *McKinsey Digital.*

Brooks, A.W. 2013. "Get Excited: Reappraising Pre-Performance Anxiety as Excitement." *Journal of Experimental Psychology.* HBS.

Carnegie, D. 2009. *How to Win Friends and Influence People.* New York, NY: Simon & Schuster.

Coleman, D. 1996. *Emotional Intelligence: Why It Can Matter More Than IQ.* London: Bloomsbury.

Duhigg, C. 2014. *The Power of Habit: Why We Do What We Do in Life and Business.* New York, NY: Random House.

Fisher, R. and W. Ury. 1991. *Getting to Yes: Negotiating Agreement Without Giving In.* New York, NY: Penguin Books.

Foley, N. July 2, 2019. *Last Orders? The Decline of Pubs Around the UK.* House of Commons library. https://commonslibrary.parliament.uk/last-orders-the-decline-of-pubs-around-the-uk/.

Gartner. 2020. "The Future of Sales, Transformational Strategies for B2B Sales Organizations." *Gartner for Sales.*

Gartner. October 21, 2021. "(Re)building Key Account Programs for Growth." *Gartner Research.*

Gartner. 2022. *Key Account Management.* Sales Glossary. https://www.gartner.com/en/sales/glossary/key-account-management-kam-. (accessed December 31, 2022).

Greenberg, M. 2016. *The Stress Proof Brain.* Oakland: New Harbinger Publications, Inc.

Grove, H., K. Sellers, R. Ettenson, and J. Knowles. August 1, 2018. "Selling Solutions Isn't Enough." *MIT Sloan Management Review.*

Hatch, M.J. 2018. *Organization Theory: Modern, Symbolic, and Postmodern Perspectives.* 4th ed. New York, NY: Oxford University Press.

Hennessey, H.D. and J.-P. Jeannet. 2007. *Global Account Management: Creating Value.* Chichester, UK: Wiley.

Holden, R.K. 2012. *Negotiating With Backbone: Eight Sales Strategies to Defend Your Price and Value.* New York, NY: Pearson FT Press.

Hughes, T. and M. Reynolds. 2016. *Social Selling: Techniques to Influence Buyers and Changemakers.* 1st ed. London: Kogan Page.

Isaac A. and J. Deutsch. February 22, 2021. "How the UK Gained an Edge With AstraZeneca's Vaccine Commitments," Politico. www.politico.eu/article/the-key-differences-between-the-eu-and-uk-astrazeneca-contracts.

Kraljic, P. September 1983. "Purchasing Must Become Supply Management." *Harvard Business Review.*

Majumdar, S. August 17, 2020. "Top 5 Distinct Sales Personas and How They Fit in Your Business," Veloxy. https://veloxy.io/top-5-distinct-sales- personas-and-how-they-fit-in-your-business/.

Mehrabian, A. 1971. *Silent Messages.* 1st ed. Belmont, CA: Wadsworth.

Mehrabian, A. and M. Wiener. 1967. "Decoding of Inconsistent Communications." *Journal of Personality and Social Psychology* 6.

McDonald M. and B. Rogers. 2017. *On Key Account Management.* London: Kogan Page.

McChrystal, S., T. Collins, D. Silverman, and C. Fusell. 2015. *Team of Teams: New Rules for Engagement for a Complex World.* Portfolio/Penguin.

Megill, K.A. 2005. *Corporate Memory; Records and Information Management in the Knowledge Age.* 2nd ed. Munich: K.G. Saur Velag GmbH.

Morgan, A. and M. Barden. 2015. *A Beautiful Constraint: How to Transform Your Limitations Into Advantages and Why It's Everyone's Business.* London: Wiley.

Navarro, J. and M. Karlins. 2009. *What Every BODY Is Saying: An Ex-FBI Agent's Guide to Speed-Reading People.* New York, NY: William Morrow.

Porter, M. 1998. *Competitive Advantage: Creating and Sustaining Superior Performance.* New York, NY: Free Press.

Porter, M. April 1979. "How Competitive Forces Shape Strategy." *Harvard Business Review.*

Scott, K. 2018. *Radical Candor: How to Get What You Want by Saying What You Mean.* London: Pan Books.

Shankar, B. 2018. *Nuanced Account Management: Driving Excellence in Business-to-Business Sales.* London: Palgrave Macmillan.

Stewart, G. 2012. *Successful Key Account management in a Week: Be a Brilliant Key Account Manager in Seven Simple Steps.* Teach Yourself series. London: Hodder Education.

Stone, D., B. Patton, and S. Heen. 2010. *Difficult Conversations: How to Discuss What Matters Most*. New York, NY: Penguin.

Sutton, J. February 23, 2018. "10 Techniques to Manage Stress and 13 Quick Tips." *Positive Psychology*.

Van Belleghem, S. 2015. *Digital Becomes Human: The Transformation of Customer Relationships*. Croydon: Kogan Page.

Vernon, C. 2017. *The Less Stress Lifestyle*. UK: Headline Publishing Group.

Vivek, S.D., S. Beatty, and R.M. Morgan. April 2012. "Customer Engagement: Exploring Customer Relationships Beyond Purchase." *The Journal of Marketing Theory and Practice* 20.

Walsh, J.P. and G.R. Ungson. January 1991. "Organizational Memory." *The Academy of Management Review* 1, no. 1.

Woodburn, D. and M. McDonald. 2011. *Key Account Management: The Definitive Guide*. Chichester, UK: Wiley.

About the Author

Marc Pettersson's career spans over two decades, from R&D to sales, from startups to Fortune 500 companies. His hands-on experience as a key account manager served as the inspiration to write the book. He is now working as an independent interim manager in commercial roles and chairman of the board of two companies. Marc is also an active angel investor and partner with MassChallenge, a global nonprofit startup incubator.

Index

Printed in the USA
CPSIA information can be obtained
at www.ICGtesting.com
LVHW020001251124
797314LV00005B/52